THE *Information* *S*uperhighway

Martin Gay
and Kathlyn Gay

TWENTY-FIRST CENTURY BOOKS
A Division of Henry Holt and Company
New York

Twenty-First Century Books
A Division of Henry Holt and Company, Inc.
115 West 18th Street
New York, NY 10011

Henry Holt® and colophon are trademarks of
Henry Holt and Company, Inc.
Publishers since 1866

Library of Congress Cataloging-in-Publication Data
Gay, Martin.
The information superhighway / Martin Gay and Kathlyn Gay.
p. cm.
Includes bibliographical references and index.
Summary: Discusses various components of the I-Way and considers how
such a vast network might affect privacy, education, entertainment, etc.
1. Information superhighway—Juvenile literature. 2. Internet (Computer
network)—Juvenile literature. [1. Information superhighway. 2. Internet
(Computer network).] I. Gay, Kathlyn. II. Title.
HE7570.G39 1996   95-46281
004.6'7—dc20   CIP
                                                                   AC

ISBN 0-8050-3804-3
First Edition 1996

Jacket design by James Sinclair
Interior design by Kelly Soong

Printed in Mexico
All first editions are printed on acid-free paper ∞.
10 9 8 7 6 5 4 3 2 1

E
570
639
1996

Contents

Introduction

Yes, you've heard about the Information Superhighway—or the Info Highway, Electronic Superhighway, Data Highway, Digital Highway, I-Way, or some other term used for this electronic system. The Information Superhighway has received a lot of press coverage, and most of it focuses on the commercial aspects of interactive media and electronic communication. One example is Pizza Hut's press release that was sent to many e-mail subscribers and was published in major newspapers across the United States in 1994:

> SANTA CRUZ, Calif., Aug. 22 /PRNewswire/—Your next Pizza Hut pizza may be coming to you via the Information Superhighway. Pizza Hut announced today that it has begun testing a new Internet ordering system which will allow computer users to order pizza and beverages through their computers for home delivery.
>
> The system, PizzaNet, is available through the World Wide Web portion of the Internet, and will provide users with a variety of product and price information through a simple, user-friendly interface.
>
> "This could be the next big step in the pizza delivery business," Jon Payne, Pizza Hut's MIS Director of Point-of-Sale Development, said. "There's a huge, untapped market of computer users who are looking for different and exciting ways to use the Internet. PizzaNet will certainly appeal to them."

PizzaNet provides product descriptions, determines if the customer is in a Pizza Hut's delivery area, prices the order, and routes the order to the proper store. It is available to Santa Cruz customers by entering this address on the computer:

`http://www.pizzahut.com`

This test of a new marketing strategy is a prime example of what many feel the new Information Superhighway will be: one huge electronic home shopping service. The hype seems to indicate that such a prediction is true. After all, who hasn't heard about the projected five hundred TV channels, video-on-demand services, pagers, cellular phones, Prodigy, and now PizzaNet? Electronic technologies are going to make it possible for some entrepreneurs to sell you these or similar products and services as well as many new ones.

Although many government agencies, educational institutions, and nonprofit organizations provide a great variety of free information via electronic technology, commercial interests have offered and will continue to offer many of the roadside attractions as the construction of the data highway continues. Businesses have developed imaginative ways to detour the public into its electronic drive-through lanes.

This book will consider a few of the products and services that you may be buying in the years ahead. Pizza is just an appetizer. The potential for applying new digital communication technologies is much greater than shopping electronically, however. It can also provide many free services to help us deal with massive changes that are taking place in schools, the workplace, the home, the government, and many other areas of society.

Information Overload

Because of rapid changes in almost every aspect of life, the world at the end of the twentieth century may be an uncomfortable place for some. But change does not have to be and is not always unpleasant; it can be exciting and challenging when we understand what is happening around us.

Driving much of the change in today's world is the massive increase in information. Some experts estimate that today we are exposed to four hundred times more bits of information than were people who lived during the last century. Certainly, the Information Age, as this data-intensive time is known, can be a very demanding and confusing period. The military, for example, has found that fighter pilots flying aircraft with advanced technical instruments experience periods of information overload during the course of intense missions. As a result, pilots may fail to hear or see important signals, so some have turned off certain warning systems in order to gain a sense of control over all the incoming information.

Information overload in everyday life is a direct result of communication technologies that have been employed so successfully over the past four decades. The media have become so pervasive in the industrialized world that those who provide the content to a large extent control what we read and see, passing on their version of reality. End users have been passive consumers of megadoses of information—although that has started to change, particularly as teachers like Ed Murphy at Bell High School in Long Beach, California, show students how to deal with the information overload. Murphy helps students distinguish between video images that are strictly advertising hype or stereotypes and those that represent the real world. His students learn the origins of images by producing their own videos, editing them to create a videotape yearbook and school video portfolios on CD-ROM.

The application of digital technology has made the personal computer (PC) a tool that is increasingly being used in schools and is becoming a fixture in more than half the homes in America. Data transfer capabilities have boomed, and now, instead of just being able to consume information from various media, we can produce information for others' consumption, contributing to a new Communication Age.

No one is sure exactly when this new Communication Age began, but it is certain that we are headlong into it today. George Gilder, a visionary and critic who reports on the telecommunications revolution, theorizes that computing power doubles every eighteen months, hence making machines less and less expensive and putting them into the hands of more and more of us. Gilder predicts that television and telephone companies as they exist today will no longer be our prime information carriers. Instead, networked computers will be the medium of the future—a developing infrastructure that could be called the roadbed of the Information Superhighway. It is being built, and most of us will be affected.

We have a choice, of course. We can remain firmly planted in the twentieth century, ignoring the potential and power of the Communication Age, but the Communication Age won't ignore us. The Information Superhighway (or the I-Way as it's sometimes called) is coming to our neighborhoods, and people could be dominated by it if they fail to understand the power of communication. If we start acquiring knowledge and skills that give us a voice in this time, even if it is a voice that allows us to make the best choice when ordering a pizza, the chances of being controlled and overwhelmed by the avalanche of information are lessened. We can emerge from this uncomfortable transition as better informed, more secure, and highly empowered citizens.

This book can be your tour guide for a trip down the data highway of the twenty-first century. We will make stops at many of the popular points of interest and take occasional side trips to some out-of-the-way places.

Fasten your seat belt. Backseat driving is encouraged.

If the younger generation is indeed the key to our future, it may be that one of the planet's most perplexing problems—freeway congestion in Los Angeles—can be remedied yet. . . .
—America Online/*Mobile Office Manager*

1

---

*D**igital Reality*

Date: June 1994

Source: America Online/Mobile Office Manager

Subject: Who's Gonna Drive You Home?

Eighteen-year-old Kevin Chang developed a software program that automatically controls acceleration and braking in cars. An infrared sensor mounted on the front of each automobile monitors its distance from the vehicle ahead and surrounding objects. "Since computers can react faster than human beings," explains Chang, "cars can drive faster and you can fit more of them on the freeway. You can tailgate closer safely." The Institute for Transportation Studies at UC Berkeley is already knocking on Chang's door.

Perhaps Chang's great new idea as described in the America Online (AOL) electronic magazine will be a standard feature on future cars produced in Detroit. Already there are many computer devices installed in the latest models. Temperature is kept constant for passengers by an environmental computer. Other information processors determine when injectors should shoot fuel into piston chambers. Mechanics can't even adjust the new engines without first reading the output of their shop's diagnostic computers. Eighty years after the Model T, Henry Ford probably wouldn't recognize today's high-tech vehicles.

Automotive technology is only one place where information has been used to transform a product. A little closer to home, the American Standard people have developed a "smart bathtub," in which "the bather selects the temperature, humidity, music, air, and water flow with the touch of electronic buttons. The unit has a communications linkage that allows its owner to contact the tub from a remote location and ask it to have the right environment ready at a certain hour,"[1] according to Stan Davis and Bill Davidson, authors of *2020 Vision*.

Distributing Information

Most of us are frequently surprised and sometimes amazed by the reports of fantastic new products and services being tested and marketed for every aspect of our lives. However, we seldom think about the way the methods for delivering the reports have changed.

Long ago, messengers delivered news by word of mouth or handwritten documents. Then new communication technology spawned newspapers and magazines that could be delivered by motorized vehicles, trains, and airplanes. Continued advances in technology made radio, telephones, and television common delivery systems for information.

Today the personal computer is a common fixture in the workplace and the home. An estimated 60 percent of U.S. households will have computers by the year 2000, and electronic networks and various online services (such as America Online, CompuServe, Delphi, and Prodigy) link computers and users around the world. Information can be distributed rapidly to millions of people, although there are fears that the vast majority worldwide who do not have access to computers will not be able to obtain the information available, as is discussed in chapter 10.

One of the best online news delivery services is *Edupage*, a free newsletter developed by a consortium of leading colleges and universities known as Educom. There are other computer network newsletters that are similar, but most just reprint the quick, interesting news bites that first appear via *Edupage*. A few examples in the *Edupage* format, which include sources, describe recent innovations in information technology:

COMMERCIAL ZAPPER

The Arthur D. Little consulting firm has developed the technology for a device that can detect and eliminate commercials; it finds a commercial by sensing blank frames and sound-level dips that precede and follow it. God bless Arthur C. Little. (Source: *Atlanta Journal-Constitution*, Bill Husted, 2/3/94, C2)

PRINT YOUR OWN STAMPS (IS MONEY NEXT?)

The U.S. Post Office is testing a postage mailing center machine which allows a customer to insert money to print a single stamp sufficient for any letter or package being mailed, from 19 cents to $99.99. (Source: *Atlanta Journal-Constitution*, 3/5/94, A13)

"PAPERLESS" JET

The new Boeing 777, the largest twin-engine plane ever built, was designed entirely on computer screens and assembled without mockups. The first "paperless" jet line, the plane was designed with eight IBM mainframes supporting 2200 workstations. (Source: *New York Times*, 3/27/94, Sec. 3, p. 1)

SOFTWARE REPLACES SPORTSWRITERS

A $100 software program called Sportswriter is capable of churning out reasonably good sports copy by intelligently stringing together words between facts. Some 80 small newspapers in the Midwest have purchased the program and are using it to cover high-school sports events. (Source: *Wall Street Journal*, 3/29/94, A1)

DESIGNER SATELLITE ANTENNAS
Researchers at Georgia Tech have developed a satellite antenna that could double as a window shade. It consists of a plastic sheet 30 by 40 inches, with tiny antenna wires and circuits printed on the surface. (Source: *Business Week*, 3/21/94, 112)

ONLINE AT ALAMO
Alamo has opened the first Web site that allows you to make real-time online car rental arrangements. The Freeways site also provides kids' games, weather reports and a forum for drivers to exchange information, such as tips on restaurants and scenic routes. <http://www.freeways.com> (Source: *Miami Herald*, 6/20/95, A6)

PARLIAMENT ON THE INTERNET
Canada's Parliament has signed onto the Internet. Computer users can now tour Parliament online, learn about parliamentary procedure, and read transcripts from committee meetings. They will not, however, be able to send e-mail to Members of Parliament or Senators; some MPs have tried it and have been deluged with messages and their staff have been unable to keep up with the mail. <http://www.parl.gc.ca> or <gopher://gopher.parl.gc.ca> (Source: *Toronto Globe & Mail*, 6/21/95, A2)

Along with *Edupage* articles, a great variety of other media sources have delivered information about electronic products and services, such as the $16,000 electronic camera that the Associated Press is using. The camera records pictures on a computer disk instead of film, and it is used at major events like the Oscars so that the pictures can be put on the wire service immediately. Apple Computer already sells a digital camera for the consumer market with a price tag of $750. Although no one expects digital pictures to completely replace film in the near future, digital cameras will become more common as prices come down.

Other newsworthy innovations in the digital world include a new type of fingerprinting. After an electronic scanner "reads" the fingertip, the information is "mapped" to a display screen, where it can be printed or transformed into a bar code for storage.

Digital technology is becoming increasingly important in medicine. Surgeons are learning their skills with the Phantom, an instrument that can be used in a "virtual reality" training session to give medical students the feeling of actually holding a scalpel and making "virtual" cuts in a patient.

Digital Technology

All of the products and services just described would not be possible without the coding of information in digital format, a complex concept that does not necessarily have to be mastered to study the effects of the technology. According to Grolier's digital multimedia version encyclopedia,

> In a digital system, the representation of a natural phenomenon is made by measuring dynamic qualities of the phenomenon at discrete moments in time. The numeric values obtained in such measurements are then usually translated into base-two values. The digital approach to recording or describing the behavior of natural events differs from that of analog technology mainly in this consideration of time. In analog technology, time is continuously observed, whereas in a digital technology, time is sampled.[2]

What does all that mean? Perhaps analyzing the use of analog and digital technology in musical recordings will clarify the concept.

Up to about fifteen years ago the most common method of storing music for easy playback was the vinyl phonograph record, a pure analog option. In that process, a band went into a studio to record a tune. Microphones were positioned to pick up the sound waves created by the instruments. The microphones converted the sound-wave energy into electronic current, which was eventually sent to a mastering device. That device controlled a needle, which bounced up and down into a spinning disk, laying tracks that were absolutely "analogous" to the movement of the sound waves created by the band. Referring to the definition, the information sampling (measuring) was real-time and continuous.

The sound storage device in common use today is the compact disc (CD), which also holds information on a coated spinning plate. That information, however, is in the form of the 1s and 0s of binary code. When Pearl Jam records an album, the process of capturing the sound waves is much the same as that for converting the Beatles' output thirty years ago. Microphones change the wave energy to electric pulses in an analog translation: the electric output is physically related to the sound information generated, and all the information is used. But then another step is added before storage takes place. Monitors are used to sample specific parts of that electrical information, which is then turned into a data code. These "bits," as they are called, are the binary language of the digital domain. It is no longer analogous to the original music, but the representation of Pearl Jam's output is still very accurate.

String after string of these data bits (code) are then laid down onto the compact disc, taking up much less space than the phonograph record needed to capture the same amount of music. The advantage of the digital data is manyfold. The information can be compressed to take up even less space. It will replay the thousandth time exactly like it played the first time. And if the manufacturer chose to do so, data could be transmitted over phone lines from the home office to any retail outlet that had a machine capable of writing information to a compact disc on-site, or to a concert hall where different machines could convert it directly back into sound waves, or send it straight into your home via the Information Superhighway.

Members of the Association of American Publishers have decided that they must become actively involved in the deploy-
ment of online information distribution systems, or get left
behind in the dust.

—Chronicle of Higher Education, *June 23, 1995*

2

Distributing Information

Years before he became vice president, Albert Gore Jr. of Tennessee
proposed that the U.S. government take the lead in seeing that important information was more readily available to its citizens. In 1979,
when he was a U.S. senator from Tennessee, he proposed a network of
"information superhighways," basing his concept on ideas he had
heard in the U.S. Congress during the 1950s. At that time, his father,
Albert Sr., who was also a senator from Tennessee, was debating how
to physically connect the main population and commercial centers of
the nation via improved roadways. The younger Gore was on hand in
committee chambers when the architecture of the Interstate Highway
System was created. In order to define his mechanism for information
exchange, he returned to the experience of that successful government program.

Gore began an inquiry into how new technology might be used
to free the flow of data so that people could become more productive,
efficient, and successful. Over the years, many academic institutions,
libraries, and government agencies had accumulated and stored vast

amounts of information. These data archives, however, have generally not been accessible to the individual who wanted to do research that might add to the nation's body of knowledge. In an article for a 1991 issue of the *Futurist*, Gore wrote:

> The United States could benefit greatly—in research, in education, in economic development, and in scores of other areas—by efficiently processing and dealing with information that is available but unused. What we need is a nationwide network of "information superhighways," linking scientists, business people, educators, and students by fiber-optic cable.[1]

Two years later, in a speech on telecommunications, Vice President Gore stressed the problem of what he has consistently called "ex-formation." He defines this as "information that exists outside the conscious awareness of any living being but that exists in such enormous quantities that it sloshes around and changes the context and the weight of any problem one addresses." As Gore pointed out,

> No matter what your field, you have to resign yourself to the fact that a great deal will take place completely outside your awareness.
>
> Take the Landsat example. We're trying to understand the global environment, and the Landsat satellite is capable of taking a complete photograph of the entire Earth's surface every two weeks. It's been doing that for almost 20 years.
>
> In spite of the great need for that information, 95 percent of those images have never fired a single neuron in a single human brain. Instead, they are stored in electronic silos of data.
>
> We used to have an agricultural policy where we stored grain in Midwestern silos and let it rot while millions of people starved to death. We now have an insatiable hunger for knowledge. And the data sits rotting away—sometimes literally rotting by remaining unused.[2]

Slow Beginnings

In the late 1970s and early 1980s, one would have to be a wild-eyed visionary or a myopic computer nerd to imagine a digital network that was capable of the functions Gore foresaw in his Information Superhighway. Because visionaries are generally in short supply and computer experts tend to stay out of political debates, the reaction to Senator Gore's 1979 proposal was less than enthusiastic. As Gore noted years later, "the only person I could find who was really enthusiastic about it was a gentleman from Corning Glass," a company that had helped develop fiber-optic technology—transmitting light through glass fibers.

This technology seems to have the most potential for transferring data over the Information Superhighway, sending and receiving digitally coded information through the transmission of light pulses, which is many times faster than sending communication signals over traditional copper wire. For example, it would take two thousand years to send the entire collection of the Library of Congress over copper wires, but only eight hours to transmit the same amount of data over a single fiber strand, according to a GTE spokesperson.[3]

This type of communications technology also provides a broad bandwidth, which can be likened to the diameter of a water hose: the larger the diameter, the greater the volume of water flow. Thus, fiber-optic cable is ideal for all data transfers, which is the reason Gore mentioned it for the Information Superhighway. That is also the reason Corning Glass was very interested in his proposal—the company was hoping to expand the market for its product.

But communications companies—cable, broadcast television, and telephone—weren't excited about the possibilities that Al Gore outlined. They were making substantial profits using their old one-way technology, and they knew that they would have to make the investment in infrastructure if the Information Superhighway was going to be built. The federal government estimates that the cost of the new two-way system will be between $50 billion and $100 billion over a ten-year period.[4] Some private estimates run as high as $500 billion if the info-road is to have an off-ramp at every house in America.[5]

Providers intend to sell services to pay for costs, but there is general agreement that government must also be involved. As some communication industries are deregulated to encourage investment in the I-Way infrastructure, some government controls are also needed to prevent consumer costs from soaring.

The Commercial Vision

Nearly fifteen years after Senator Albert Gore made his proposal about disseminating information, science, technology, the economy, and politics changed. In 1993, Senator Gore became vice president of the United States, an excellent position from which to champion his I-Way proposals.

The idea had become fashionable, and as far as business was concerned it was possibly very lucrative. Engineers had increased the capabilities of the tiny PC to beyond what the original mainframe computers had been able to accomplish. At the same time, prices of the machines had dropped steadily, and millions of households had been equipped, becoming digitally connected via networks.

Within the past few years, the communications companies have awakened to the fact that the Information Age is here. Businesses expect to make money by packaging information in a manner that is highly accessible to the buying public.

How can they make information accessible? By selling products and services to consumers in their homes before they get into the car to head for the mall on the old type of highway. Someone has to take the information services to the consumer's door—provide the means for the data transfer—and the one who gets there first reaps big profits.

For business, the Information Superhighway became the digital door-to-door salesperson who could knock at the buyers' computers or the interactive TVs of the future. Delivering interactive consumer services and developing new profit centers became the vision for the cable industry and the telephone industry (which recently started using the term *telephony* to better describe its expanded capabilities). Both industries are developing the technology to send digital information through their lines.

Cable serves at least sixty million U.S. residences (it's within reach of 87.4 percent of all residences in the United States), and coaxial lines have broader bandwidth capabilities than old telephone lines.[6] But copper phone lines have other advantages. They already go into 98 percent of homes in the United States, and two-way capabilities are built in. The narrow bandwidth of phone lines is the major problem in making the current phone system the main branch of the I-Way.[7] The race is on to see which system will be the first to refit and begin to provide the types of services that the public will want to buy.

Broadcast TV and radio will also become major players in determining the way the data highway is finally manifested. Digital technology is providing these media with tools that can be highly effective two-way communicators. Wireless devices such as satellites, cellular telephones, and pagers are other tools that will play important roles on the superhighway as various services combine technology; computers with video services and telephony with information services are two examples.

The days of distinct segments in the telecommunications industry are probably over, although in September 1995 the giant AT&T company stunned the business world by separating into three distinct businesses: one to manufacture large computer systems rather than personal computers, another to make communications equipment, and a third to offer communication services such as cellular and long distance.

At the same time, other companies have merged. One example is Microsoft, which has joined film producers to form an interactive media company. Another is the merger of CBS with Westinghouse Electric Corporation. And Time Warner bought Turner Broadcasting System, bringing together a major entertainment company and a cable television empire. The CBS-Westinghouse and Time Warner–Turner mergers will provide opportunities for the companies to expand in the interactive media markets.

One of the reasons for new corporate partnerships is the fact that the investment any *one* company can make in the infrastructure (cables, fiber optics, switchers, connectors, set-top boxes, routers, computers, software) is not enough to lay even the roadbed for the Information Superhighway. The costs have to be distributed among numerous enterprises.

Another factor has been the sixty-year-old federal communications law, which (until recently) was designed to keep one segment of the industry from competing with another, forbidding, for example, telcos from providing video service to the home. However, in June 1995, Congress passed a bill that provides for some deregulation of telephone, cable TV, and broadcasting companies. As a result, supporters say, communication companies should be able to compete in each other's markets. A cable provider or telco might enter the movie delivery market, for example. This competition is expected to benefit communication industries, but critics charge that it could result in higher consumer rates for use of communication services.

There is one more reason for new mergers in telecommunication. Whoever is going to offer a service to the public will need content, such as old movies and television shows, and a means to produce new ones. Disney, Paramount, and other production companies have these products, thus they are desirable partners for phone, cable, and broadcast providers, although copyright laws and how they apply to multimedia are still under study and are highly controversial. Copyright regulations are likely to develop as cases are brought to court.

Experimenting and Testing

Business interests are now experimenting with and testing the types of services that they eventually will deliver on the I-Way. Cable companies, for example, are developing the mechanisms that will allow subscribers to use their computers to gain online access to commercial services and the Internet through cable TV wires. Steve Case, chief executive officer of America Online, says "there's no reason the things being done in the CD-ROM world couldn't be done on-line"—such as downloading text files from remote sources and then adding sound and pictures faster than can be done from a disc.[8] Charges for such a service would be based on the time actually used, logged digitally, while online via the computer.

Experiments are underway with prototype networks that will connect between 50 and 7,000 consumers to test everything from the set-top boxes, which will be the first interface for the digital signals, to the types of movies people will be demanding. Ray Smith, Bell Atlantic's chairman, believes that someday telemedicine, telelearning, and other "society-transforming" services will be available, but right now he needs to find a "killer application" like video-on-demand, direct-response advertising, and interactive games to pay for the development.[9]

Interactive Network tried the games idea in Chicago, San Francisco, and Sacramento. Signing up with their network allowed a person at home to play along with the regular contestants on *Jeopardy* and *Wheel of Fortune*. The Sega Channel hoped to be in twelve U.S. cities and in Canada, distributing new downloadable versions of their games each month.

However, because of money problems and lack of cash flow, Interactive Network announced in June 1995 that it was forced to suspend its interactive game testing, laying off 80 percent of its work-force. Apparently, there was not enough public interest in their in-home interactive device, which according to critics, is fairly primitive hardware and too expensive for a broad base of viewers. In addition, the software required to activate the hardware is too advanced for most users.

Nevertheless, U.S. companies have been investing millions of dollars to produce components such as remote control devices for multimedia networks and sound boards that recognize speech commands, which will have a role in the interactive days ahead.

Numerous companies now manufacture or are developing high-density compact discs that provide up to 18 gigabytes (one gigabyte is one billion bytes) of data capacity on two sides and single-sided multimedia discs with a storage capacity that allows viewers to watch up to four and one-half hours of their favorite movies without flipping the disc. The high-density discs can be adopted for a variety of applications, such as research, interactive entertainment, business and finance, and online storage.

Companies also continue to experiment with interactive entertainment. U S West Marketing Resources in Los Angeles is developing GOtv, an interactive entertainment service, which will include information about movies and local restaurants and events. Consumers will be able to access the free service using their home television set, a set-top box, a remote control, and a telephone. An opening screen will include a news feature about the entertainment industry and GOtv specifics, which viewers can watch, or with a remote control they can choose one of three categories: movies, dining, or events. According to a company news release:

> Once a category is selected, a short entertainment show for that category will appear. Again, viewers can interrupt this show at any time and control what happens next by making another selection or by asking for more information. . . .
>
> An additional feature on GOtv will be a movie ticketing option. Viewers may choose to purchase movie tickets by calling a central ticketing number provided by MovieFone and customized for the GOtv application. Viewers will call the number and enter a numeric code displayed on the television screen to order tickets. . . .
>
> U S WEST is [also] developing spots for interactive advertising embedded in the context of the entertainment information that will enable national advertisers to build product/brand image and measure consumer reaction to electronic direct response advertising.
>
> Ads will also be interactive, allowing consumers to ask for more information about a product or service. By clicking on the screen, viewers

will select and navigate through categories of advertiser information that will include full-motion video clips. These interactive ads will give consumers information on how to get samples, coupons or additional product-specific information to help their purchase decision. . . .[10]

Another vision of how a multimedia application might work was described in the *Seattle Times*, a newspaper serving a region known as the "biotech belt," where more than 600 computer software companies are located. Since April 1994, one section of the Sunday edition of the newspaper has been devoted to "Personal Technology," and in October 1994 staff columnist Paul Andrews projected what could happen with interactive technology by the year 2000:

You've settled down in your living room to watch the NBA playoff game between the Sonics and the Trail Blazers.

You tell the screen, "NBA playoffs," and a wireless link connects a large flat-panel screen on your wall to America Online, an electronic information service. On comes the game.

You've missed the first five minutes. No problem. You say "Open replay window" to your screen and fast-forward digitally through the action so far.

The first image is the national anthem, a multimedia reproduction of Jimi Hendrix's Woodstock rendition. . . . You fast-forward ahead to a crashing dunk by Shawn Kemp and, using the remote as a pointer, click on a Kemp Watch button on the screen. You get Kemp's vital statistics, minutes per game, season scoring average, plus elevation off the floor for the dunk.

You get news stories about Kemp from all over the planet: What the Atlanta Constitution columnist is writing about Kemp, what they're saying in the Italian league, the latest from the Shawn Kemp Fan Club in Elkhart, Ind [Kemp's hometown]. . . .[11]

No one is certain, of course, that the above scenario will materialize, and not everyone will be interested in all of the possible information that could be included in such interactive programming. In some instances, huge amounts of data are distracting (as was discovered with fighter pilots), and in the case of sports fans a lot of extraneous information may be considered overload.

Yet the information overload and the complexity of some technologies have not dampened the enthusiasm of engineers who design multimedia and other electronic systems for the Information Age. As Robert W. Lucky, a research executive with AT&T, pointed out in the early 1990s during a speech to the National Academy of Engineering:

> Few of the engineers who developed the videocassette recorder imagined that every town today would have a video rental store. The inventors of optical discs concentrated on video applications, never guessing that compact audio discs would displace vinyl records . . . we make progress where none is expected. Unaware that cities are a hopeless cause, we design successful urban transportation systems like BART in San Francisco or the Washington Metro. Oblivious to the hopelessness of the educational crisis, we pursue technological aids to education.
>
> This single-minded pursuit of solutions may be hopelessly naive for the world of the future, and there's no question technology can produce bad outcomes as well as good ones. But . . . I believe technology increasingly will free us to focus on matters more worthy of our human intellect, producing a world in which art, religion, music and philosophy coexist with amazing technical advances. Technological products are only tools, and they can be used to make life less, as well as more, stressful. The real solution to our frazzled lives lies not with rejecting technology but with harnessing it in new ways to manage information overload, quiet the beepers and calm our nerves. We need to retain faith—not so much in technology as in our own power as humans to make it work for ourselves.[12]

The good news from Washington is that every single person in Congress supports the concept of an information superhighway. The bad news is that no one has any idea what that means.

—*Rep. Edward J. Markey, chairman of the House Subcommittee on Telecommunications and Finance*

3

*T*he NII and Government's Role

It is impossible for the Information Superhighway to be constructed without the business sector, and businesses make decisions based on the bottom line—whether or not there will be a profit after expenses are paid. Companies want to make money, and that simple fact has driven a great deal of change and has enhanced the way of life for many people. Yet commercial interests may not necessarily make decisions that benefit as many people as possible.

As plans for the I-Way have continued to develop, Vice President Gore pointed out the need for a business-government partnership, using a story about the sinking of the *Titanic* nearly a century ago. In his view, the story "tells us a lot about human beings—and telecommunications." Gore explained that just a few hours before the *Titanic* collided with an iceberg, other ships were sending out warning messages about the dangers of heavy pack ice. After the collision, "*Titanic* operators sent distress signal after distress signal," but only a few ships responded. Why? Gore noted that investigations proved:

The wireless business then was just that, a business. Operators had no obligation to remain on duty. They were to do what was profitable [usually transmitting messages from wealthy passengers]. When the day's work was done . . . operators shut off their sets and went to sleep. In fact, when the last ice warnings were sent, the *Titanic* operators were too involved sending those private messages from wealthy passengers to take them. And when they sent the distress signals operators on the other ships were in bed.

Distress signals couldn't be heard, in other words, because the airwaves were chaos—willy-nilly transmissions without regulation. The *Titanic* wound up two miles under the surface of the North Atlantic in part because people hadn't realized that radio was not just a curiosity but a way to save lives. Ironically, that tragedy resulted in the first efforts to regulate the airwaves.

Why did government get involved? Because there are certain public needs that outweigh private interests.

Today, as divers explore the hulk of the *Titanic*, we face a similar problem. A new world awaits us. It is one that can not only save lives but utterly change and enrich them. And we need to rethink the role of government once more.[1]

The National Information Infrastructure

In September 1993, the federal government released a paper outlining the role it should take in the development of the I-Way. Government being what it is, the name chosen to explain the concept had to be more "official" sounding than "Superhighway." So the title of the vision became "The National Information Infrastructure: Agenda for Action." The NII initiative, as it is now known, is the formal declaration of goals that Vice President Gore and many others expect to achieve with the Information Superhighway.

According to the federal government's position, the I-Way, or the NII, should be built, owned, and operated by private enterprise, but some government officials want to do what they can to support its development. The Agenda for Action outlines how this can best be achieved, while taking into consideration the needs of private citizens who want to be information consumers but not enhanced couch potatoes. Some of the key points follow.

In developing our policy initiatives in this area, the Administration will work in close partnership with business, labor, academia, the public, Congress, and state and local government. Our efforts will be guided by the following principles and objectives:

- Promote private sector investment, through appropriate tax and regulatory policies.
- Extend the "universal service" concept to ensure that information resources are available to all at affordable prices. Because information means empowerment—and employment—the government has a duty to ensure that all Americans have access to the resources and job creation potential of the Information Age.
- Act as a catalyst to promote technological innovation and new applications.
- As the NII evolves into a "network of networks," government will ensure that users can transfer information across networks easily and efficiently.
- Ensure information security and network reliability. The NII must be trust-worthy and secure, protecting the privacy of its users.
- Protect intellectual property rights. The Administration will investigate how to strengthen domestic copyright laws and international intellectual property treaties to prevent piracy and to protect the integrity of intellectual property.
- The Administration will seek to ensure that Federal agencies, in concert with state and local governments, use the NII to expand the information available to the public, ensuring that the immense reservoir of government information is available to the public easily and equitably.[2]

Responsibility for implementing these objectives is the mandate of the Information Infrastructure Task Force (IITF), created by an executive order of President Clinton. The IITF is made up of representatives of the United States Departments of Commerce, Defense, Justice, and State; the General Services Administration; and other government groups. The makeup of the task force underscores two important facts: information technology is almost overwhelming, and it cuts across all aspects of life.

In order to obtain public input about the I-Way, President Clinton also ordered the formation of a NII Advisory Council. This group is made up of representatives of the print media, television, radio, computer industry, telcos, cable, education, public interest groups, and others. Members meet to discuss their constituents' visions of the NII in order to feed this information back to the government.

The only K–12 education representative on the council is Bonnie Bracey of the Arlington, Virginia, school district. She took the imaginative step of creating an electronic mail discussion group that is open to anyone with a computer and a modem. In other words, the discussions are not private, and they are open for public viewing and participation. Some seven hundred members of the NII-TEACH group are providing her with a broad base of experiences and ideas that she has been able to take to the NII Advisory Council.

Online Projects

The Agenda for Action paper includes examples of ways the NII can be used by all Americans to create jobs, spur economic growth, reduce health care costs, access lower-cost government services, prepare young people for the new workplace of the twenty-first century, and build a more open and participatory level of democracy. Many projects are already in the planning stages or are up and running:

■ May 1993, Governor Jim Hunt announced the creation of the North Carolina Information Highway, a network of fiber optics and advanced switches capable of transmitting the entire 33-volume *Encyclopedia Britannica* in 4.7 seconds. This network, deployed in cooperation with BellSouth, GTE, and Carolina Telephone, is a key element of North Carolina's economic development strategy.

- In California's Silicon Valley, academics, business executives, government officials, and private citizens are working together to build an "advanced information infrastructure and the collective ability to use it." A nonprofit organization, Smart Valley Inc., is helping to develop the information infrastructure and its applications. Many business applications include desktop videoconferencing, rapid delivery of parts designs to fabrication shops, design of chips on remote supercomputers, electronic commerce, and telecommuting.

- The Texas Telemedicine Project in Austin, Texas, offers interactive video consultation to primary care physicians in rural hospitals as a way to alleviate the shortage of specialists in rural areas. In the state, more than seventy hospitals have been forced to close since 1984. The Telemedicine Project has increased the quality of care in rural areas and has provided at least a 14 percent savings by cutting patient-transfer costs and provider travel.

- InterPractice Systems, a joint venture of Harvard Community Health Plan in Boston and Electronic Data Systems, has placed terminals in the homes of heavy users of health care, such as the elderly, pregnant women, and families with young children. Based on a patient's symptoms and medical history, an electronic advice system makes recommendations to HCHP's members about using self-care, talking with a doctor, or scheduling an appointment.

- The Heartland FreeNet in Peoria, Illinois, provides a wide range of community information to the citizens of central Illinois twenty-four hours a day. Topics covered include 113 areas of social services, a year-long community calendar, the American Red Cross, current listings from the Illinois Job Service, resources for local businesses, and local government information. Experts in all fields from the law to the Red Cross to chemical dependency volunteer their time and expertise to answer questions that are anonymously asked by the public.

- The Big Sky Telegraph, in operation since 1988, is an electronic bulletin board system linking Montana's 114 one-room schools to one another and to Western Montana College. The system enables "virtual communities" to form and connects schools, libraries, county extension services, women's centers, and hospitals. In addition, Montana's high-school students learning Russian can communicate with Russian students, and science students are participating in a course on chaos theory offered by the Massachusetts Institute of Technology (MIT).[3]

The I-Way Today

Clearly, much of what is envisioned for the National Information Infrastructure is beginning to develop. As you read this book, the structure of the Information Superhighway is on the drawing boards of many different telecommunications companies. Just as telephone companies, cable providers, and the wireless industry have been testing and prototyping at a furious pace to create an infrastructure to sell goods and services, so has the Network of Networks been growing at an astounding rate.

Many experts believe that the Internet, or the "Net" as it is called by frequent users, is the best example of the beginnings of the NII. Is it the Information Superhighway? Not yet, if the I-Way is defined as the medium of interactive video exchange.

But consider this. If you want to communicate with a friend or colleague 2,000 miles away in two minutes or less; or you want to see pictures of the latest eclipse taken minutes before; or you want to check on jobs available in any area of the United States; or you need to buy a CD, flowers, books, teddy bears, software, computers, cars, guitars, or whatever; or you would like to send a singing birthday greeting to your mother's computer in Indiana, then the Internet is a super place to travel.

Applications that make the Internet easier for the average person to use are introduced weekly, and companies are constantly developing new ways to use information services and the Internet. For example, the Oracle and Intel partnership has produced real-time, interactive video through the telephone lines, and that technology is becoming increasingly common throughout the United States. Multimedia elements have been added to established online services like America Online, CompuServe, and Prodigy, and they are certainly part of the new AT&T and Microsoft online services.

Across the United States, banks will soon be part of interactive services with the aid of software that allows customers to use their personal computers somewhat like automated teller machines. Software producers such as Microsoft and Intuit already are aligned with major banks, the first step toward making it possible for customers to transfer cash and trade stocks while in their own homes or offices.

One company, First Virtual Internet Payment System, has established the world's first electronic bank. It is described by its developers as "a financial services company created specifically to enable the global buying and selling of information by anyone with access to the Internet." Users do not have to buy additional software or hardware to use the service. Based on existing technology, First Virtual (FV) provides users with a safe link between the Internet and banking and credit card operations. A customer can register with FV and make online purchases using their FV account number.

According to the company, "All transactions are confirmed with the buyers before being posted . . . to the credit card processing company over separate, secure, dedicated lines that are not accessible from the Internet. Credit card numbers are never sent over the network, thereby eliminating the need for encryption [the use of a coding system] and the potential for fraud." Customers pay a small fee for registration and a service charge for each transaction and sellers pay processing charges.[4]

A similar service is DigiCash, which invented the technology that has been used at highway toll booths where customers pay tolls from their moving vehicles. The Amsterdam-based company explained:

Electronic cash is based on the increasingly used cryptographic systems for "digital signatures. . . ." One such system involves a pair of numeric keys that work like the halves of a codebook: messages encoded with one key decode with the other key. One key is made public, while the other is kept private. By supplying all users with its public key, a bank can allow them to decode any message encoded with its private key. If decoding by a user yields a meaningful message, the user can be sure that only the bank could have encoded it. These digital signatures are far more resistant to forgery than handwritten ones.

In the basic electronic cash system, the user's equipment generates a random number, which serves as the "note." His equipment then "blinds" the note using a random factor . . . and transmits it to a bank. In exchange for money debited from the user's account or otherwise supplied, the bank uses its private key to digitally sign the blinded note and transmits the result back to the user. The user's equipment unblinds the note, which it later pays with. The payee checks that the note's digital signature is authentic and later sends the note on to the bank, who in turn checks the signature and credits the payee accordingly.[5]

Perhaps it will be five to ten years before the I-Way comes into your life through the latest in interactive appliances. But there's no reason to wait and dream about the info-world. If you have a driver's license for the Internet, you can tour that highway and get a glimpse of what the future is likely to hold.

The Internet is already an information superhighway, except that . . . it is like driving a car through a blizzard without windshield wipers or lights, and all of the road signs are written upside down and backwards.

—Dave Barry

The Information Maze

Called the Network of Networks, the Internet is often described as if it were a tangible "thing." But the Internet is not a network service, an organization, or a commercial enterprise, although it contains elements of those entities. The Internet actually has been evolving for almost three decades, beginning with an experiment in data communications undertaken by the United States Department of Defense (DOD) in 1967.

Because of international tensions and fears of armed conflict, the DOD needed a communication system that would assure continued connections between their "command and control" structures in the event of a nuclear strike. The plan was to construct a system in which various types of computers could communicate with one another and not be controlled from one particular point. In that way, the loss of one branch of the system would not affect the operation of the other branches. A network was eventually established to meet this requirement, connecting four university computer sites: University of California at Los Angeles (UCLA), Stanford Research

Institute, University of California at Santa Barbara, and the University of Utah in Salt Lake City.

Vint Cerf was a graduate student at UCLA when the Defense Advanced Research Projects Agency funded an inquiry to determine how best to transfer information along its experimental network, known as ARPANET. Cerf is credited with developing the software that allowed computers connected to a local area network (LAN) to "talk" to any other machines likewise connected. As Cerf explained:

> By 1971 there were about nineteen nodes in the initially planned ARPANET with thirty different university sites that ARPA was funding. Things went slowly because there was an incredible array of machines that needed interface hardware and network software. We had Tenex systems at BBN running on DEC-10s, but there were also PDP8s, PDP-11s, IBM 360s, Multics, Honeywell . . . you name it. So you had to implement the protocols on each of these different architectures.[1]

If you are not a computer network programming expert, you may find Cerf's explanation somewhat confusing. Suffice it to say that it took many years and endless hours of effort by many people to perfect the seamless structure of data transmittal.

By the mid-1980s, Cerf's packet-switching software, which divided streams of data into small addressable bundles called Transmission Control Protocol/Internet Protocol (TCP/IP), became the common language of the networks. Today there are more than one hundred applications, or "protocols," in the TCP/IP protocol suite that do specialized tasks such as sending e-mail, transferring files, and allowing real-time chats, searches, and monitoring. Some of these protocols will be covered in later chapters, but the important point is that it does not matter which type of computer you use to access the I-Way of today.

All computers are relatively easy to set up for accessing information. Because of this, many new smaller networks, some of which are made up of only a few dozen users, have linked themselves to the chain of networks that is the Internet.

No "Home Office"

The original ARPANET is no longer alive; it became extinct in 1990. Even before that time, in 1984, the National Science Foundation (NSF) had taken the initiative for improving the capabilities of the Internet structure for research and education. The Internet's bandwidth capabilities were increased, and new, faster computers were put online. The U.S. government provided funds to develop and improve the technology that fueled the spectacular expansion of the system. Some traffic, especially for education and research, still uses the NSF facilities for transfer, but the bulk of Internet activity has now been rerouted to commercial providers.

Other large networks, known as "backbones" because of their large bandwidth capabilities and heavy traffic flow, also comprise major sections of the Internet. For example, there is the Australian Academic and Research Network (AARNet) and the NASA Science Internet (NSI). The Swiss operate the Swiss Academic and Research Network (SWITCH). However, even with the massive transmission capabilities of these large wide area networks (WANs), not one of them is the Internet "home office."

The National Science Foundation can set some standards for the type of information that moves over the NSFNet, but there is no real structure in place that allows them to police data that might move among other individual networks of the global Internet. Why? Because the technology itself diffuses the authority. Cerf designed it that way. Every party can, and does, function independently.

Small or large networks are connected to the Internet through a computer on the particular network that is loaded with the TCP/IP protocol suite. That machine creates a node, or gateway, to the Net. One node connects to another node that is itself connected to a node of other connected nodes of the Internet. In other words, you attach your link to any other link, and presto! you are on the Internet, too. The connection does not have to be approved by a central authority. You simply obtain a feed of information from a machine up the line. The software that runs the whole system is the only government of the Internet. Each node is equal to all others in that sense.

New nodes must have appropriate names so that packeted messages can find their marks, but no committee, guru, or Internet god has to give permission. Data encoded with a valid address will find its way to the correct address in any manner it can. For example, once out of the home computer, the packet can move over a phone line, link to a satellite, shoot across space via a cellular link, and come back to earth just down the street from the sender. Other paths are also available.

Setting the Stage

In the beginning, ARPANET was set up as a linking device between what were then mainframe supercomputers at a few university and government installations. The infrastructure allowed a community of scientists and scholars from various parts of the country to work together, almost as if they were in the same location. Computing power was in such short supply in the early 1970s that it was critical for these machines to work on scientific problems together. Researchers used the network to log on to a remote computer where they could check data, retrieve files, and leave messages for other scientists. Human nature being what it is, the heaviest use of the new network evolved toward the latter—leaving messages. Electronic mail quickly became the users' favorite new tool.

Soon software was available that enabled a sender to post a message once and have it distributed to many members of a group with common interests. Other methods were developed to enhance personal communication, too. Network newsgroups were formed so people could discuss a wide variety of topics, most of which were no longer related to the original ARPANET goals of scientific inquiry. In fact, people were using the new computer and network resources and tools to communicate on matters of personal interest from favorite baseball teams to episodes of *Star Trek*. The genie was out of the bottle; people had discovered the real value of digital networking.

Communications. Community. News. Free exchange of ideas. These are the services and ideals that have driven the growth of the Internet. David Clark, senior research scientist at MIT's laboratory for computer science, explained it this way:

> It is not proper to think of networks as connecting computers. Rather, they connect people using computers to mediate. The great success of the Internet is not technical, but in human impact. Electronic mail may not be a wonderful advance in Computer Science, but it is a whole new way for people to communicate. The continued growth of the Internet is a technical challenge to all of us, but we must never lose sight of where we came from, the great change we have worked on the larger computer community, and the great potential we have for future change.[2]

Incredible Growth

In 1969, there were four Internet nodes, or hosts. Few could have predicted just how broad the Network of Networks would become in the succeeding years. Today there is a global web of thousands of computer networks, with an estimated forty million people able to connect to the Internet—a number that is growing rapidly. Reporting on the growth of connectivity in a July 1994 speech, Anthony-Michael Rutkowski, executive director of the Internet Society, put this expansion into some perspective:

> If the first stage took us to 2000 hosts over the first ten years, and the second stage scaled the connectivity from 2000 to 1 million over eight years, the third state of Internet growth is now marked by host counts that will likely proceed from 1 million to 100 million [by the year 2000].

We are literally watching it grow before our eyes. . . . Many smaller local backbones have experienced regular traffic increases of 20 percent per month.

The core Internet's massive size, high performance, and open connectivity has proved a magnet to nearly every other kind of computer network. . . . These peripheral networks create a larger Matrix Internet that . . . provides many millions of people with lowest common denominator Email connectivity. In this capacity, the Internet is truly the world's universal electronic messaging backbone.[3]

NSFNet is currently phasing out its role as backbone provider, and it will concentrate once again on scientific and research applications. There is a great deal of speculation about what will fill the void left by NSFNet. In its NII visions, the federal government sees business as the answer. Indeed, that may be the case, since businesses are not waiting for broad bandwidth technology to set up their kiosks along the Information Superhighway. Smart concerns are beginning to see the potential of Vint Cerf's dream.

5

New Tools of the Trades

Since at least 1980, hundreds of companies have used computer networks to facilitate communication within their own organizations.
The heaviest commercial Internet users are Exxon, Transamerica,
GTE, Unisys, Texas Instruments, Boeing, and Motorola.[1] Several of
these companies operate more than 200 local area networks that are
connected to the Internet.

The LANs can connect managers, employees, support personnel, independent contractors, vendors, research agencies, and other
critical personnel who happen to be located within a particular area.
That area might encompass anything from a section of one floor in a
high-rise building to many buildings and thousands of computers over
several miles. Specially configured computers, known as routers, then
make the connection to the Internet so that an employee using a
computer on, for example, one of Exxon's more than 260 different
networks, can make a connection on a network that is thousands of
miles away.

In addition to using computers for intracompany communications, businesses are connecting to the Internet to obtain information, ranging from news about breakthroughs in science to customer complaints, which can help improve a product or service. According to a report in *Fortune* magazine, most companies that have connected to the Internet "boast of increased productivity, better collaboration with strategic partners, and access to what is in essence the world's largest public library for a seemingly infinite range of information. But the Internet is virgin territory when it comes to true commerce . . . most large companies have just begun to see the Internet as a potential marketplace."[2]

Nevertheless, some companies are communicating with customers linked via the Information Superhighway. Pizza Hut, for example, understands that making its products available on the Internet is good business. First, the establishment of PizzaNet was reported throughout the world. Pizza delivery on the Information Superhighway translated into a good story and lots of free advertising. Second, by beginning the process early and on a small scale, the corporation will be in an excellent position to implement broader services in a wider geographic area when the I-Way is finally used by the majority of Americans.

It will take time to develop a new way of doing business through the Internet. Many questions will need to be answered: how to advertise, what products and services should be sold, how money will be collected, and so on. One of the first decisions that Pizza Hut and any other business must make is determining what type of protocol (software) it will use to inform consumers about its services.

The Internet speaks the language of TCP/IP, as was discussed in the last chapter, and there are several protocols that take advantage of that fact. Should you feel a need to better understand the protocols, technical books and papers on the subject abound on and off the Internet. For this book, it is possible to present only a sampling of the protocols and Internet tools, such as electronic mail (e-mail), gopher, and World Wide Web (WWW).

Electronic Mail

Adam Engst explains the most basic and most used of the Internet protocols, e-mail, in his primer on connectivity, the *Internet Starter Kit*:

> Almost everyone who considers himself connected to the Internet in some way can send and receive email. Most personal exchanges happen through email, and email handles most *directed information*, or information that is directed only at the recipient. Email also carries a great deal of *undirected information*, or information that is geared for a group of people but for no one person in specific. Most of this undirected information travels in the form of *mailing lists* or *LISTSERVs* (a special form of mailing list software used by numerous discussion lists). In these discussion lists, all the readers can post questions, answers, and comments, and everyone can read everyone else's postings. . . . Email is also the medium for automated requests for information.[3]

The automated capabilities of e-mail also allow people to subscribe to newsletters. An acclaimed online newsletter about Macintosh computers is *TidBits*, written by Adam and Tonya Engst. By sending the proper e-mail message to the computer that runs the *TidBits* subscription database, software is automatically activated to add the sender's name and e-mail address to the distribution list. A welcome message with important information about how to "unsubscribe" and use various commands is immediately sent back to the new subscriber.

TidBits is just one of many electronic publications available through electronic mail. Most are free to subscribers who have an account that can receive Internet e-mail. Many are subsidized by commercial concerns that either include a small ad or a mention of the sponsoring business. Some have begun to charge a fee for delivery, just like magazines that come through the regular mail. Subjects include general news topics, sports, art, and especially computer and communications (Internet) issues. There is even an automated-response newsletter called *Net-Letter Guide*, published by John M. Higgins. He reviews some of the free publications online, such as *NSF Network News*, which Higgins calls "the real nuts and bolts of the net." To learn about *Network News* or to subscribe, e-mail to the following address:

```
To: newsletter-request@is.internic.net
Subject: Ignored
Body: Subscribe NSF Network News
```

Certainly, if you have not seen an e-mail address before, it appears confusing. But in the Net world, and to automatic list-processing software, it makes a great deal of sense. To translate: Send a message by typing the address **newsletter-request@is.internic.net** in the "To" position of your e-mail message. Leave the "Subject" line blank. (There is an exception, however. Some software requires a subject, and a "dummy" word must be typed in to send the message.) Place the exact words **Subscribe NSF Network News** in the body of the message. In a short time, you will start seeing the *NSF Network News* in your own "In-Mail Box."

Another popular newsletter already described is *Edupage*, which can help you deal with information overload. You can subscribe by sending an e-mail request to

listproc@educom.edu

After you fill in the address, the subject line can be blank or filled in with dummy words. In the body of the message, type only the following: **Sub Edupage (your name)**—that is, type in your actual name, without the parentheses. Send the message, and the *Edupage* computer will pick up your e-mail address from your message and automatically reply, accepting your subscription and giving you further instructions.

If you want to subscribe to Higgins' *Net-Letter Guide*, send e-mail to

```
listserv@netcom.com
```

The body of the message should read: **Subscribe net-letter.**

There are two other methods you can use to access newsletters. For example, to reach *NSF Network News*, you can use these addresses: gopher to

```
is.internic.net: About InterNIC Information Services/
NSF Network
```

or WWW to

```
http://www.internic.net/newsletter
```

Gopher and WWW (World Wide Web) are two of the most popular methods people use to navigate on the Internet. (One note of caution: sites change frequently, as do their addresses, and some move or are no longer available.)

Gopher

Developed by the University of Minnesota (home of the Golden Gophers) as a way to distribute campus information to students and staff, gopher is used to "go for" information. It is able to "burrow" into unseen sites and retrieve and display data more fully than the FTP (file transfer protocol) it was designed to replace. Again, if you need detailed information on FTP or gopher, refer to one of the fine reference books on how to get around the Internet.

The one thing that you should know about gopher, however, is its ability to bounce the user all over gopherspace (computers anywhere around the world running gopher software) and access information in real time. In contrast to electronic mail, which sends a message to an individual or a machine for an expected response sometime in the future, gopher sends commands to a properly configured "server" computer. That computer should provide an instantaneous response. If you use gopher from your machine to connect to one of the many commercial servers running that software, such as **market-place.com** of Boulder, Colorado, you can choose to download or display information immediately.

A connection to **marketplace.com** will allow you to see a file that explains what the service provides. Downloading to the connecting computer will enable you to import the text into a word processor, where it can eventually be formatted, as has been done with the text that appears below:

> Marketplace.com is the Internet Information Mall created and operated by Cyberspace Development of Boulder, Colorado. The objective is to provide a useful service to the Internet community by offering a convenient environment for online shopping. We also want to provide a useful service to businesses that want to offer such products and services on the Internet but do not wish to set up and operate a full-scale Internet server.

A little more exploring within this site reveals the Online BookStore and this associated introductory file:

> The Online BookStore (OBS) offers to the Internet public electronic versions of current books. Since 1992, we have established working business models for publishing on the Internet, and paying royalties to authors and electronic rights holders for the titles we make available online. Readers can freely browse catalogs, book descriptions, sample chapters, and free information, decide what to buy, clear their credit card, and download books . . . to their machines for personal use.
>
> Accessing books at this site can be a fully electronic experience; you can browse free of charge all gopher-accessible documents. To access the for-pay items, you will need a gopher+ client [this is enhanced Gopher software that allows the user to input text information to the OBS server computer] on your machine. Here's how it works:
>
> Select the item you wish to buy and you will be prompted for your credit information. After filling in the required information you will be given access to the items you purchased. To download an item select it

and press the **Return** key. You will then be prompted for a filename to save the item. For text files you will need to press **s** for **Save** to initiate the download.

After you have established an account (which can be done on-line using another TCP/IP protocol called Telnet), you can order a traditional bound copy from a catalog of many titles. The book will be sent immediately to your home. Or, if you don't want to wait for the U.S. Postal Service, you have the option of downloading (for a fee) some of the titles directly to your computer. Print a book using any typeface you happen to like. Or save it as a text file on your machine for browsing and searching as the need arises.

What if you want to find a book that the Online BookStore doesn't carry? Gopher to the University of California at Irvine bookstore at **gopher.cwis.uci.edu** or try Pathfinder Press at **gopher. std.com** Also, there is Wordsworth Books of Cambridge, Massachu-setts, at this address: **gopher.wordsworth.com**

There are many other bookstores as well as many other services selling products with the aid of gopher. Finding them is not always easy, but Dave Taylor's "The Internet Mall: Shopping on the Information Highway" is a free mailing list (newsletter) service that can be of help to the brave cybershopper. Other sources can be found by accessing World Wide Web.

World Wide Web

Along with commercial services, numerous government and other nonprofit services are available through World Wide Web and an ad-dress known as Uniform Resource Locator (URL). World Wide Web, often called the "Web" or "3W," was developed at a high-energy re-search center in Switzerland called the CERN, whose name in English stands for the European Laboratory for Particle Physics. It at-tempts to bring all the other protocols together under one system.

By using a software tool called a browser, you can read text and then go to other linked references, which may be additional text on the topic, graphics, or sound (recordings). With a Web browser, consumers can already access gopher servers and FTP sites. One popular product on the market is Netscape by Netscape Communications. Some free browsers include Mosaic, developed at the National Center for Supercomputing Applications, EINet's MacWeb, and WinWeb. Services such as CompuServe, Prodigy, America Online, EcoNet, and the new AT&T and Microsoft online services also provide browsers for WWW access.

The real advantage of the Web is its ability to link pictures, videos, sounds, text, software, and any other digital information with the click of a mouse button. All the other protocols up to this point have been text based. That is, the interface between you and the information you retrieve has been strictly in alphanumeric format. It has been impossible to see a picture or to hear an audio recording using gopher. That all changed with "HTTP," or hypertext transfer protocol, which is the basis of the World Wide Web. Now, when you reach a site with HTTP software (a browser) running, the results will look something like the screen image that appears on page 47.

Like other WWW access points, this is known as a "Home Page"; it is similar to a magazine's table of contents. From here, you can navigate to other hyperlinked files by clicking on one of the buttons or highlighted terms or phrases shown. For example, you can see an image of the first family or the White House, or you can read a welcome message from the president or vice president of the United States. When you select the button or term you want, the software will be directed to bring up that linked page.

If you access a commercial service, such as an online store or catalog, there are likely to be numerous options from which to choose. Perhaps you decide to select and download three pages of images showing products that you can view later. Or you might want to see what is available right away, so you click on a specific item. Immediately, a new page is displayed, with pictures of products and their prices.

Now you have the option of going back to the catalog page,

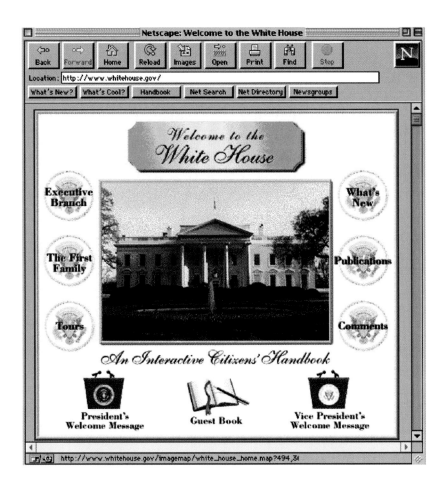

choosing another product area to visit, ordering a kite, or logging off and saving your money for another day.

The Protocol of Choice

Public and commercial Home Pages just described use only a fraction of the WWW capabilities and represent only limited examples of the types of goods and services that are offered on the Net. Others include the Mammoth Records site, where visitors can download album cover graphics, audio recordings, and even videos of their favorite band's latest singles. Want to hear Leonard Cohen read a poem? It's there for a free download, too.

Travel planning is a popular service available on WWW, and a person can gather travel information from computers located around the globe. A traveler in Japan planning to visit San Francisco, for example, can access the San Francisco Reservations Home Page at

```
http://hotelres.com/
```

There you can do a search for available rooms in a hotel, motel, or bed-and-breakfast. The search can be limited according to price, location, and type of accommodation.

Anyone looking for an apartment in New York City might be able to find one by accessing **http://www.nyrealty.com/** This free service lists nearly 3,000 apartments and homes for rent or for sale. Such services are also available in other cities and towns. For example, you can actually see houses or other buildings for sale or read listings such as those that appear on this Home Page, as shown on page 49, at **http://www.olympus.net/realestate/winderpt/prop**

The National Association of Realtors predicts that by the year 2000, databases across the United States will be linked so that a person in Indiana, for example, can shop for a retirement home in Florida, a vacation home in Colorado, or a dream home in Hawaii. It is not certain, however, whether real estate shopping will be done primarily from a home computer, through interactive television, or at a kiosk in a shopping mall.[4]

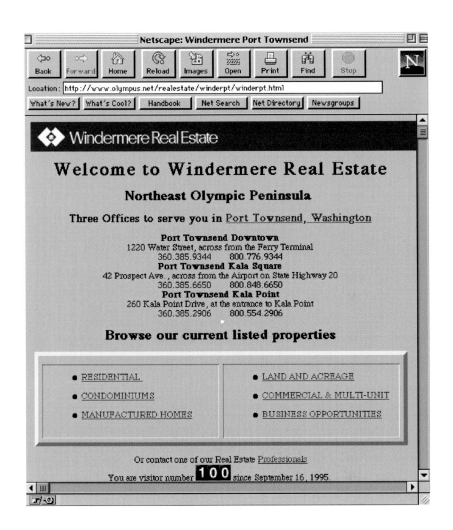

There appears to be no limit to the way entrepreneurs may use the new electronic tools of the future. Those tools are also being used with increasing frequency by students, political groups, nonprofit charity organizations, environmental activists, and numerous other individuals and groups, as described in subsequent chapters. Meantime, though, you may want to take a break from reading and give yourself a treat. Pizza anyone?

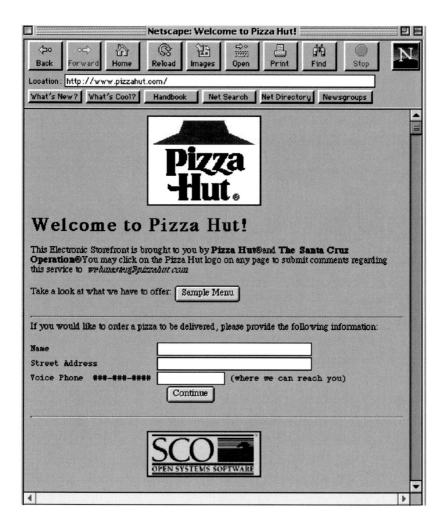

Today, we have a dream for a different kind of superhighway that can save lives, create jobs and give every American, young and old, the chance for the best education available to anyone, anywhere. I challenge you . . . to connect all of our classrooms, all of our libraries, and all of our hospitals and clinics by the year 2000.

—*Vice President Al Gore*

6

The One-World Schoolhouse

On a global scale, students from the elementary to postgraduate level are making use of online services and the Internet to enhance their education. In November 1994, the Associated Press reported that a major medical teaching tool on the Internet—a computerized cadaver—was unveiled at the annual meeting of the Radiological Society of North America in Chicago. Called the "Visible Man," the three-dimensional images were prepared from photographs and X rays of 1,870 cross sections of an executed prisoner's body. The prisoner had been sentenced to die by lethal injection for a murder and had requested that his body be donated to science.

The cadaver images were compiled in a huge program that is stored at the National Library of Medicine and may be downloaded free via Internet if the library grants permission. However, there is so much data that downloading takes about two weeks of nonstop time and more than thirty personal computers with typical amounts of storage would be needed to hold the program. Obviously, Visible Man will be used primarily by medical schools and research specialists with appropriate computer facilities.[1]

On a less grand scale, several dozen universities offer online classes through computer networks, and many more will be doing so in the future. In the United States, a few universities offer degree programs but most offer only a small number of online courses. Students in Africa, Asia, or Europe can use a computer, modem, and communication program to take a class in the United States, and vice versa.

How is this possible? Students connect to a university's computer, where lectures, reading lists, assignments, and sometimes classroom discussions are housed, waiting to be accessed. Tests or discussion questions may be answered publicly on a class bulletin board or by e-mail to the instructor.

It is not unusual for online teachers to live far from the universities with which they are affiliated. A University of Phoenix (Arizona) instructor, Ken White, who teaches human relations and business communications, lives in Everett, Washington, but conducts online classes for students from across the United States.

At the moment, no one expects online classes to replace traditional teaching on university campuses—or at elementary and secondary schools. But many educators do believe that this type of learning will supplement and expand educational opportunities, as it already has for some schools with access to the I-Way.

The First Elementary School On-ramp

On March 15, 1994, sixth-grade students at Hillside Elementary School in Cottage Grove, Minnesota, switched on a Macintosh computer running software that allows anyone with an Internet connection to access information about their school. On that day they made history, becoming the first elementary class in the world to build their own on-ramp to the Information Superhighway. Working in conjunction with the University of Minnesota College of Education, the school's stated goal was to "incorporate use of the resources on the Internet into the curriculum of elementary school students and to have students participate in creating resources" that others could access on the Internet.

To reach Hillside's World Wide Web site, access a favorite browser and type in the URL (WWW address):

`http://hillside.coled.umn.edu/`

After connecting, you may see an image of the school, which can be downloaded for later viewing, or you might see a picture of balloons lofting skyward to illustrate that the school is "beginning to soar on the Internet" as the caption states. If you choose hyperlinked text with the mouse's pointer, you may reach a page that has a listing of links to the students' own pages that have been created since the project began. Choosing one will bring up the page of an individual who has taken the time to write an introduction and include a favorite photograph or piece of computer-generated artwork.

Pick a link called **Internet Research Projects** and a page of new choices is presented. You can pick any of the different research papers that have been prepared by students using resources available on the Internet. The students have covered subjects ranging from dinosaurs to virtual reality. They have made their work available to other students who might find those topics interesting or are researching for a homework project, whether they reside in the same town or across the world in China.

Other Schools on the Net

Since the Hillside School on-ramp appeared, countless other elementary, middle, junior high, and high schools have become part of the networked world. The schools have set up either WWW or gopher servers to deliver information.

In Boulder, Colorado, for example, K–12 students of the Boulder Valley School District have created a monthly newspaper called *Vocal Point* that is distributed on the Internet at

`http://bvsd.k12.co.us/schools/cent/Newspaper`

According to its introductory text, "The newspaper creates a forum in which the youth of Boulder can express their ideas and be heard . . . throughout the world." Each month, the newspaper covers a significant topic—the June 1995 issue, for example, focused on censorship, with articles on school dress codes, book banning and selection, censorship of violent and sexual music lyrics, pornography, sex and violence in the movies, and censorship on the Information Superhighway.

In Indiana, the department of education is in the process of helping all of its 295 school districts set up WWW sites. Greenwood Middle School, in Greenwood, a town near Indianapolis, has a WWW page designed by its students that has links to an audio greeting from the high-school principal and another to the school song. If you access the Home Page for Riley High School in South Bend, you can link to its electronic store, where students and science teacher John Webbins offer science programs that can be downloaded. One Riley student, Derek Carr, has developed an ecology program that shows what happens to farmland when it's left untilled and reverts to its natural state. "I took pictures of a field in different stages of succession and put them in the computer," Carr explained. "I'm trying to put together a computer slide show."[2]

The schools that have established computers to welcome "incoming" inquiries from around the world are only a small part of the total number of schools that have begun the complicated process of providing an Internet connection for their students and staff. In some cases, one phone line hooked to one computer on the initiative of a single teacher is the sole extent of the connectivity. At other sites, like the pioneering Issaquah schools of Issaquah, Washington, the entire district is networked, providing Internet connectivity for 4,000 students and a staff of 1,400. That type of connectivity is expanding rapidly throughout the United States, where it seems that virtually every school district is developing a new technology plan to help in the overall effort to restructure education. Those plans almost always include a component recommending Internet access.

The Port Townsend, Washington, school district is a good example of the type of effort that is going on nationwide today. Located on a relatively remote, rural section of the Olympic Peninsula about two hours (via ferry boat) from the high-tech mecca of Seattle, this creative community of 7,000 is in the beginning stages of taking the expensive turn onto the Information Superhighway. In 1992, the citizens voted to fund a Technology Bond of more than half a million dollars. That money was earmarked for new computers, TVs, VCRs, and other equipment. There was no thought then of creating a digital network to enhance communication within the district's four schools and to the greater community or the world. After all, there were two phone lines coming into the site. Teachers and parents had gotten used to jumping into the car to catch up with their colleagues or their kids' instructors.

Then a new superintendent was appointed. Dr. Gene Medina, an experienced administrator from another part of the state, had seen what had been accomplished in Issaquah, Washington. There, a small group of enlightened parents who were familiar with the new digital communications skills necessary to compete successfully in the modern workplace volunteered to coordinate the development of a district-wide LAN. They wanted their kids to have access to the tools of the modern world.

In Port Townsend, Medina recommended that his new district put a hold on spending any of the bond money until they could take a close look at the Issaquah experience. One year later, after much planning and discussion, and with the help of many community members, Port Townsend schools were poised to go online. Some $500,000 was dedicated to making a network and a connection with the rest of the world. This effort is only the beginning, however. More computers must be purchased, teachers have to be trained, and students have a lot to learn about how to use the Information Superhighway—just like their peers nationwide.

More Connections

Since the latter part of the 1980s, computers and Internet connections have been proliferating in classrooms, partly due to the attempt to reform the way schools function and the way students learn.

Electronic technology helps increase student comprehension, and students have access to a great deal of free information and services via the Internet.

Suppose you need to get information about dinosaurs for a school project. Certainly you would use printed sources—encyclopedia, books, magazine articles, and so forth—which you would find in a school or local library. Before going to a public library, however, you might be able to go online to access its electronic catalog to find out what print materials are available. On the Internet, there is likely to be an electronic listserv in which subscribers discuss this subject, and messages can be downloaded for reference. Or if the school has an Internet connection that will support the HTTP, or hypertext transfer protocol, otherwise known as the World Wide Web, you could access

`http://ucmp1.berkeley.edu/expo/cladecham.html`

You would be greeted with this message: "Welcome to the Hall of Dinosaurs." Then you would be informed that you are in an antechamber, and

> ahead stretches a series of long hallways where you can see various amazing skeletons. In front of you is a map. It is not your usual map. It is a map that paleontologists use all the time to understand how animals are related to each other through time. This map is called a cladogram. It will help you navigate the hallways in a logical and progressive way. This cladogram is particularly special because you may navigate through the various hallways of dinosaurs with it. Clicking on the text parts of the cladogram will magically transport you into various hallways.

Perhaps you want to know about the Hubble Space Telescope and observations of a spectacular collision of two solar system bodies. In July 1994, the comet Shoemaker-Levy 9 collided with Jupiter. You could learn about the effects of that impact by accessing

`http://newproducts.jpl.nasa.gov/s19/s19.html`

More than 30,000 students have participated in a science project called Monarch Watch via the Internet. It began in 1992 when high-school science teacher Brad Williamson in Olathe, Kansas, convinced Orley Taylor, a University of Kansas entomologist, that students could help gather data about the fall migration of monarch butterflies. In his research, Taylor is attempting to find out what routes the butterflies take from Canada and the northern United States to their wintering spots in Mexico. He also wants to know why and how the monarch butterflies select the same roosts along the way—one of which happens to be just outside the high school where Williamson teaches.

In order to collect data, butterflies had to be tagged, and a request went out over the Internet for help. Teachers and students in thirty states responded, and through messages on the Internet they learned how to capture butterflies, tag them, and report their sightings. The project has helped students "learn science by doing science," according to Williamson, who noted that when his students first became involved "they kept asking questions. They started noticing every butterfly that moved, even though that wasn't the original idea. They started to develop an awareness of the natural world."[3]

If you want to learn more about Monarch Watch you can find its site at

```
http://129.237.246.134/
```

You will be able to see a logo—a monarch butterfly with binoculars—and link with articles that describe what is known about monarch migrations and their life history. You can also read messages from people who have seen monarchs and other information related to this research.

Following are descriptions of some other well-developed resources that might be helpful for learning in the new style or for a school research project. The URL for each site, accessible via a web browser, is provided with each entry.

Item 1

You can explore a variety of topics through KIDLINK, which is based in the United States but is electronically maintained in Norway. KIDLINK is a grassroots project designed to get as many young people as possible between the ages of ten and fifteen involved in global dialogue via the electronic medium, beginning with Kids-90 and continuing each year since. At the start of Kids-96, more than 40,000 young people from seventy-two nations on all continents had taken part in various communication formats—from individual dialogue to classroom participation.

Students may take part in Internet Relay Chats (IRCs) conducted on computers in real time. For example, a person at a computer in a U.S. or Canadian classroom types in a message on a screen, then another person a block away or around the globe at another computer types in a response, and users at still other locations can join in the chat at any time.

You can read about other tasks undertaken when you access KIDLINK at a site that can be reached at

```
http://www.kidlink.org
```

Item 2

The Interactive Frog Dissection is a site that was originally designed for use in high-school biology classrooms, and it is considered a valuable preparation tool or even a useful substitute for dissecting a frog in the laboratory. It includes movies, so it is necessary for those accessing the site to have that video capability on their computer. The site is

```
http://curry.edschool.Virginia.EDU/~insttech/frog
```

Item 3

"Welcome to Le WebLouvre in Paris! I wish you the most pleasant visit," is how Nicolas Pioch, curator of the world-famous art museum in France, would welcome you if you use this address to access:

```
http://mistral.enst.fr/~pioch/louvre/
```

Once there, you can follow the hyperlinks and see online exhibits such as a French medieval art demonstration or a collection of well-known paintings from famous artists. Or you might tour Paris, the Eiffel Tower, and the Champs-Elysees. You can even click on icons that will bring you some background music for your visit.

Item 4

So you want to visit the South Pole and learn about the Arctic Circle? Use this WWW address:

```
http://www.deakin.edu.au/edu/MSEE/GENII/NSPT/NSPT
   homePage.html
```

Once on site, you will learn that

"The New South Polar Times" is a bi-weekly newsletter written by one of the staff at the Amundsen-Scott South Pole Station, South Pole, Antarctica. The idea for the newsletter grew out of correspondence between several of the staff at the Amundsen-Scott Station and participants in an Internet workshop sponsored by the Virginia Space Grant Consortium during the summer of 1994.

The workshop leader, Katie Wallet, and the officer in charge of NOAA operations at the station, Lt. Tom Jacobs, decided that students and teachers from around the world would be interested in learning about Antarctica, the scientific research which was taking place at the station, and life at the station. Realizing that communication with individual classes was prohibitive because of the busy schedule of the staff at the station, they decided to create the newsletter, which would be made available on Internet. Lt. Jacobs volunteered to write the newsletter until he left the station.

The title, "The New South Polar Times," was suggested by Lt. Jacobs and named for the first newsletter to be written in the Antarctic, "The South Polar Times" a newsletter for and by the men on Robert

Scott's ship, the *Discovery*, on Scott's first expedition to Antarctica, July 1901–September 1904. It was on his second expedition to the Antarctic that Scott lost the race to the South Pole to Roald Amundsen by just 34 days. The station at the South Pole is named for these two brave men.

One of the hyperlinks takes you to a description of McMurdo, which is the largest station at the South Pole and home to about a thousand research scientists and staff during the summer months from October to February. Then you can learn about Palmer Station, north of the Arctic Circle, and the Amundsen-Scott Station, which is 840 miles from McMurdo:

> It consists of a geodesic dome, 53 feet high and 165 feet wide, attached to steel arches extending 80 feet from opposite sides of the dome. Under the dome are modular buildings, fuel bladders storing 225,000 gallons of fuel, and heating, snow-melting, and research equipment. About 80 people live there in summer and about 20 people in winter.

Interesting and useful sites are added daily on the Net. In the near future, we will see even more. Most will be using the World Wide Web with its multiple capabilities to display their information.

Clearly, a protocol like HTTP—the World Wide Web—is an adaptable and robust tool on the I-Way. But many individuals and schools don't yet have the type of connection needed to support HTTP. That's no reason to despair, however. What many do have is the limited, but still very useful, gateway connection that gives them access to electronic mail.

In the Industrial Age, we go to school. In the Communication Age, schools can come to us.

—*header of the* Online Chronicle

7

Gathering Information by E-Mail

The good news is that even low levels of connectivity will get you decent access to the latest information being placed online. Most of these resources are using the World Wide Web to publish, but you no longer have to have a web browser to connect. In an example of the speed at which the roadbed of the Information Superhighway is developing and changing, CERN (the group who developed the HTTP software that makes the Web possible) has begun an experiment to allow retrieval of WWW pages via e-mail. They have added this automatically generated service, which is much like subscribing to newsletters, as was discussed in chapter 5, to make certain that the majority of computer users have access.

The bad news is that e-mail retrieval doesn't allow the graphics that enhance the text and are so important in the WWW interface. And it isn't as much fun as a direct connection. However, it is a very helpful option for those who don't have the latest-model vehicles for cruising the I-Way. Suppose, for example, you wanted to see the Home Page for the *New South Polar Times* (discussed at the end of chapter 6). You could send an e-mail message to the CERN computer at

listserv@www0.cern.ch

with the URL of the *New South Polar Times* in the body of the message. Then you would receive e-mail in return. The message would contain a header and introductory text such as this:

```
Date: Mon, 24 Oct 1994 05:37:38 +0100
Reply-To: listserv@www0.cern.ch
From: listserv@www0.cern.ch
To: martini@olympus.net
Subject: The New South Polar Times (URL:
http://www.deakin.edu.au/edu/MSEE/GENII/NSPT/NSPThome
   Page.html)
               The New South Polar Times
[IMAGE]
*********** DEAKIN UNIVERSITY, AUSTRALIA ************
******* THE HOME SERVER FOR THE GENII PROJECT *******
   The contents of the document under this cover are
the views of the authors and do not necessarily re-
flect the views or policies of Deakin University.
****************** WORLD WIDE WEB ******************
[IMAGE]
```

The word *image* in brackets represents the graphics you would see if you access through a WWW browser, but they are not available in the e-mail message. You would also see information about other documents you can retrieve by e-mail, as shown here:

```
INCLUDED IN THIS PROJECT ARE:
The current issue [1] of the New South Polar Times
Back issues [2] of the New South Polar Times
Lessons and ideas [3] for using the New South Polar
Times in the classroom
Information and data [4] about science at the South Pole
How you can submit questions [5] and get answers to some
frequently asked questions
```

```
Other resources [6] on the South Pole and Antarctica
A History [7] of South Pole Exploration
The Climate Monitoring and Diagnostic Laboratory
(CMDL) [8]
The Blizzard [9]
```

To navigate to other parts of the project and get information about, say, "A History of South Pole Exploration," you can send another e-mail to CERN with the reference number **7** in the body of the message. Depending on the time of day and the quantity of data traffic on the Net, the new text message should be in your e-mail In Box in a few minutes.

Other Resources by Mail

In addition to sending subscription commands to mail list computers to get electronically distributed newsletters, a user can send commands by e-mail to join other types of mailing lists. Thousands of mailing lists have been established to automatically distribute the messages of people who are connected because of a common interest. Pick a subject, *any* subject, and there is probably a mail list that will address it.

Via a listserv, as the software is known, each subscribed member of the list can write a message and send it to the listserv computer. From there it will automatically be sent to all other members of the list. That automated process is an efficient method for sending and receiving the latest information in a particular area of interest.

Unlike mail sent by a postal or delivery service, however, messages on a mail list are public—out in the ether, so to speak—and available to anyone who subscribes or has access to the mail list. Thus, people who use mail lists need to be aware that if their messages are addressed to a general audience (not part of a private message to an individual) and are not part of copyrighted material, their words probably can be used by others, although legal experts are still struggling with this issue.

Most subscribers to mail lists are not overly concerned about the privacy of their messages, however, since they usually want to share information as broadly as possible. Many people in academic fields, for example, are using the lists to discuss cutting-edge theories before they find their way to the traditional printed journals.

Do you want to know the latest thinking on how "chaos theory" relates to economic development planning? You might subscribe to "econ-dev." Or perhaps you have something of interest to add to a discussion on how the Information Superhighway will affect K–12 education? Join the "NII-Teach" list and you'll be able to give your opinions to Bonnie Bracey, the K–12 education representative of the National Information Infrastructure Advisory Council. Or you might like to take part in a discussion on sexual harassment and how to prevent it by joining Sociologists Against Sexual Harassment and their list called SASH-L.

The care of pets is a topic of discussion on numerous mail lists and on forums—versions of mail lists that are part of such commercial services as CompuServe and America Online. On one list, participants share concerns and information about golden retrievers. For example, one subscriber wanted to know what to do about a retriever's skin fungus that puzzled even the veterinarian caring for the dog. After an inquiry sent to multiple recipients of **golden@hobbes.ucsd.edu** the subscriber received several responses attempting to explain the fungus and how it might be treated.

On another mail list called Superk12, whose subscribers are primarily educators, Tom Layton of Eugene, Oregon, shared his plan for a project that would link his students in English and applied technology courses to local writing coaches via the Information Superhighway. Layton used both print and electronic media to explain his plan. First, he received permission from the *Eugene Register-Guard* to upload a feature the paper had published about his project. After the article was sent to the mail list, it was automatically distributed to all subscribers, who then could read it online or download the article to read later.

According to the news report, Layton's plan calls for students to meet in the school's computer lab, which has a direct link to the Internet. Using e-mail, students would send their classwork to mentors who would evaluate the work and return their critiques the same way. Layton hopes the program will "help create better learning opportunities for students . . . [who] need to be writing more" but they are not because the teaching staff has been reduced and "teachers don't have enough time to grade more course work." With the mentor program in place, teachers could assign more papers than they could evaluate alone. That would benefit students who would be able to "test their writing abilities and receive a dose of 'real-world perspective,' "[1] Layton said.

Because of the thousands of official mail lists functioning from computers throughout the Internet world, many sources now provide information on what topics are covered and explain how to become a subscriber. In his books on the Internet, Adam Engst includes a small sampling of lists, such as the following:

- "ev" is a list at **listserv@sjsuvm1.sjsu.edu** that deals with electric vehicles.
- "inmylife" is located at **listserv@wkuvx1.bitnet** if you would like to talk about Beatles-era popular culture.
- "kidsnet" is administered from a computer at **listserv@vms.cis.pitt.edu** and correspondence that passes through there revolves around all topics in the K–12 arena; it is for both teachers and students.
- "snes" is for people who want to trade e-mail on the Super Nintendo Entertainment System. It's at **listserv@spcvxa.spc.edu**
- "smoke-free" at **listserv@ra.msstate.edu** centers on issues of recovery from cigarette addiction.[2]

Personal Contacts

The use of mail lists as a method to keep in touch with a community of individuals with common interests often leads to making direct contact via e-mail with a specific person who is on the list. In this way, a whole new adventure may begin with someone you probably never would have met any other way.

There are tales about folks who have met online, discovered a mutual attraction, courted, and eventually married. Other stories are more sinister in nature, such as those about pornography and hate mail sent through e-mail. There is even a story about an unstable person who actually "stalked" someone through the electronic medium and prompted an investigation by the FBI. These and other problems are described in more detail in chapter 10.

However, the overwhelming number of contacts are positive. For example, on New Year's Eve 1994, there was a virtual party on a global scale. In cities from New York to Rome to London, thousands of people connected to the Internet and a chat line that allowed them to spend the evening "talking" to each other, flirting online, and generally interacting as if they were face to face at a real live party.

In another type of beneficial Internet contact, a New Hampshire man, a computer programmer, met his current business partner through e-mail. For years, the programmer had dreamed about starting his own project, but he felt he needed the talents and resources of others to make his dream come true. Then one day he posted an e-mail message to a mail list calling for submissions from writers who might want to cooperate in the development of a CD-ROM for the expanding market in home multimedia computer software. In a few days he had a response from a California woman who had similar visions about starting a CD-ROM publishing house.

Over a period of six months the two talked by telephone four times, used the United States Postal Service's "snail mail" on five occasions, and sent hundreds of e-mail messages back and forth. All this communication resulted in the establishment of a corporation, a name, and three possible products the company hopes to develop.

Countless small businesses have used e-mail to get established, and many companies already in business use e-mail for a variety of purposes. At General Electric's Research and Development division, for example, employees send and receive 5,000 messages a day. They use e-mail to exchange information on current research, to stay in touch with people working in laboratories across the United States, and to contact customers and suppliers. Such usage reflects not only the importance of e-mail as a communication tool but also one of the many ways that today's workplace is changing due to the I-Way.[3]

One of the things we used to have to do before school when I was a kid was to change the sprinkler pipes in the alfalfa fields. My best old friend Patty still changes the sprinkler pipe in the morning before she heads out for the day. She gets up, goes into the den, flips on the computer and sets things in motion in a field some 30 miles away.

—*Joni J. Rathbun, teacher*

8

*T*he Changing Workplace

One change that e-mail communication and the I-Way have brought to many businesses is the location of the workplace. Through "telecommuting," which is expanding very rapidly within some industries, some workers can complete their assignments at home or on the road. Then they e-mail reports back to the main headquarters and receive feedback the same way.

Telecommuting got a substantial boost in California after the 1994 Los Angeles earthquake. Because of the damage to the freeway system of Los Angeles County, it was almost impossible for employees to reach their normal workplaces. Frequently, there were backups of four to eight hours on the existing roads. As *Edupage* reported:

> Following the 6.8 earthquake . . . Pacific Bell offered telecommuting opportunities to its workers . . . nine months later five out of 10 employees who accepted the "telecommuting relief package" are still working from home, and almost half of those now work from home five days a week.[1]

According to *NBC Nightly News*, there were two million people telecommuting in America in 1990, but in 1994 that number grew to an estimated eight million. By the year 2001, the number of people who work in their homes and communicate with peers, managers, clients, and others via the Information Superhighway will probably be thirty million.[2]

Some businesses don't even have to have a "home office" any longer. Communication via e-mail is so fast and reliable that it has allowed "virtual companies" to organize; they exist in and between the homes and automobiles of the employees of the company.

Even if your job doesn't directly rely on the I-Way, the trend is clear: jobs in America are changing. The skills necessary to perform those jobs are different from what was expected of employees just a few years ago.

Digital literacy is the key. As a Ford Motor Company manager explained: "Maybe your neighborhood mechanic will need a computer degree to fix all that high-tech gadgetry under the hood. . . . The 'shade tree' mechanic is becoming a thing of the past."[3]

Peter von Stackelberg of Applied Futures in The Woodlands, Texas, agrees. An expert on the impact of the new technologies on employable skills, von Stackelberg writes:

> The amount of information is doubling approximately every 2.5 years. This means that between 1990 and 1995, the amount of information available increased by 4 times. . . . We can see the explosive rate of growth in the amount of information available to us on the Internet as an example. The amount of job knowledge needed in 2010 will be approximately 10 times that needed 20 years earlier. A hypothetical example is that if you needed 500 pages of documentation to repair all the vehicles that came into your shop in 1990, you would need 5000 pages of documentation in 2010 because of the increasing complexity and variety of vehicles.[4]

Training for the Workplace

Many school reformers are pushing for changes in the classroom that will address the challenges of dealing with this exploding mass of information. Consider just the information needed to repair automobiles. As von Stackelberg pointed out, an automobile repair manual would have to expand to five thousand pages in a traditional bound book, but that amount of data would fit comfortably on a single CD-ROM, with a lot of room left for video and graphics to aid a mechanic in her or his work. There will undoubtedly be a database of auto information, updated daily, accessible only through a modem. Obviously, most mechanics will need to know a lot more than how to read or use a torque wrench. They will have to use computers and an array of information devices if they expect even entry-level employment.

Business advisers recommend, however, that schools begin to teach more than how to use the new digital tools. Consultant von Stackelberg, for one, bemoans the fact that schools don't currently teach for the conditions that are now operative in the real world, where data retrieval and manipulation, cooperative problem solving, and systems consideration are the rule:

> Schools have been designed to teach skills relating to the needs of an industrial age. We are seeing changes coming in school curricula, but they are happening slowly. We need a much stronger emphasis on skills such as team work, systems thinking, and others listed as soft skills. This will require significant changes in teaching methods and the goals of school systems. . . . [Currently] the focus is often to pass a test, not learn or teach what is required to succeed in the world of the future.[5]

Von Stackelberg goes on to make some specific recommendations for schools if they want to produce students who are ready for the workplace that is developing today:

1. Ensure that all students are literate before they leave the sixth grade.

2. Ensure that all students are able to work in teams on significant projects in which success depends on the full participation of all team members.

3. Ensure that all students are "systems thinkers."

4. Ensure that all students are able to demonstrate personal leadership.[6]

Can students attending high school today meet these criteria? The changes necessary to accomplish this goal seem overwhelming at times, but there are some stellar examples of early success that are encouraging. You may already have heard of the senior at Liberty High School in Issaquah, Washington, who developed and now maintains a sophisticated data network for Windermere, the largest real estate corporation in the state.

Or you may know a teenager like Daniel Marcus who appears to be well prepared for the future. Daniel is a student at White Station High School in Memphis, Tennessee. His father, Louis, has established the Global Shopping Mall (GSM) on the Internet so that anyone with the right navigation protocols can shop for goods and services from a variety of vendors who pay to maintain "stores" on his computer. Louis has been able to provide substantial opportunities for his son, and Daniel has made the most of them. What follows is his story, in his own words, sent by e-mail.

What I Did on My Summer Vacation

I don't consider myself a genius, because I'm usually bordering on the edge of space cadet and space. But I make good grades and I usually know what's happening.

I've been using a computer since I was about 4 or 5 years old.

Mostly games to start, but over the years I've also learned typing and basic commands for DOS and most recently UNIX.

I have always had a passion for art, and it has become a major part of my life. Upon the arrival of the scanners and Adobe Photoshop program, I started to teach myself the essentials of image manipulation.

After much experimentation and with guidance from our two technicians, I became quite proficient.

Knowing what skills were required for a job with my dad, I asked to help in the production of the graphic portion of the mall. I was then given a summer job scanning, digitizing, and manipulating images for the mall.

My summer job consisted of digitally rearranging many different jewelry catalogs into one catalog which would be seen and evaluated by a potential customer in the Global Shopping Mall. The new pages I created consisted of a page from the original catalog made smaller, and a side bar consisting of blown up, detailed images of the individual links.

Not only did I get the chance to work with Adobe Photoshop, but I have experience working with Aldus Pagemaker, Textbridge, and Q-edit. . . . I have been applying the summer skills which I learned to my school projects, whenever possible. I have already found these tools are a major asset, and give me the ability to make spectacular presentations which go far beyond that which is required. I think that it will be a giant step forward in the school system when these tools become available to all students so that they can learn and grow up with them as I did.

The Internet is the other great advantage I have available to me. I play the guitar, and I have found sites on the Internet that can give me current news and music to play. I know from experience that these tools are invaluable to someone when they find out what is "out there." When I am unable to find the information I'm looking for in a reference book, my research takes me directly to the Internet.[7]

Future Job Trends

Daniel's experience will serve him well as he approaches that time when he is ready to make his own way in the world. His skills and talents are exactly the type that are expected to be in high demand in multimedia applications—an industry poised for phenomenal growth. Besides their "digital" beginnings, CD-ROMs, the projected 500 TV channels of the Information Superhighway, video games, and virtual reality applications all have one thing in common. They must have "content" and someone has to provide it. In other words, the medium of television isn't worth a dime without a show to watch. Expand that need for programming content to all of the other new media that are coming online in more and more homes and it translates into thousands of new jobs, even new job categories.

Microsoft Corporation, the software developer and one of the most successful companies ever, expects to hire great numbers of people to fill the needs of their new multimedia division. According to senior human-resources manager Denise White, Microsoft hires a lot of people with experience in product design, "but we also look for people [without experience] who show . . . promise. We'd look at any person who shows an ability to . . . design and create multimedia products." Her advice to anyone who wants to work on Microsoft projects is "to get a good education and augment it with specifics in your discipline. Attend design schools and get internships. You must be able to demonstrate creative skills and an ability to put those creations into a usable form with a computer."[8]

Programmers, graphic designers, writers, editors, and other jobs available now and in the future at Microsoft or the many new small companies popping up every day will require skills of a very advanced nature by current standards. Enablers will be needed to help people use new technology. Librarians trained to access data banks on the I-Way will be in demand. Corporations will need people who can access, manipulate, and analyze information and store it for efficient retrieval.

Don't be fooled, however, into thinking that you can avoid learning about the new technologies if you don't aspire to that type of work. Some experts predict that computer literacy will be as important in the job market as knowing how to read, write, and do arithmetic. Remember the mechanic.

In addition, the Information Superhighway will pass through a place like McDonald's. Want a job flipping burgers? It's very likely that entry-level jobs for that corporation and thousands of others will require skills never imagined just a few years ago.

The most important skill determining a person's life pattern has already become the ability to learn new skills, to take in new concepts, to assess new situations, to deal with the unexpected.

—*Seymour Papert* / The Children's Machine

9

Cyber Circus

Some computer users are learning new skills while at the same time enjoying a little relaxation. One way to do that is to get hooked to an Internet site running software that allows you to enter a Multi-User Dimension (MUD), also called a Multi-User Dungeon, named for the first program designed to play a cyberspace version of the board game Dungeons & Dragons. There are now more than 300 MUDs accessible to users of the Internet.

If you enter that virtual reality—computer-generated world— you could become part of a scene such as this one described in a *Time* magazine article, "In the Jungle of Mud":

> You're in a tropical rain forest, trying to decide whether to explore the ruined Maya temple in the distance or climb into the forest canopy overhead, where you might see some monkeys. Suddenly there's a yellow-brown jaguar sitting on the branch above you, flicking his tail from side to side, his yellow eyes fixed on yours. Maybe climbing a tree isn't

such a good idea after all. You don't think jaguars eat people, but rather than find out, you head off across the forest floor, turning this way and that, until you manage to get yourself hopelessly lost.[1]

Are you in mortal danger? "Virtually" speaking, yes, if that is the reality you choose to live at the moment. If you want out of that scene, it's as simple as disconnecting from the I-Way and getting back to your homework. The "jungle" you just left exists only on your computer.

People who are frequent MUD visitors tend to stay for extended periods in these worlds that have been created using only text descriptions. Players take on roles by creating names, physical characteristics, emotions, and actions for characters that match the realities of the particular MUD they are visiting. Suppose you want to be a brain surgeon and transplant a new personality into your boyfriend or girlfriend? MUD reality can allow you to "live" it.

The *Time* article documented a few of the different worlds that users can access to play out their roles:

> Some MUDs are fashioned after medieval villages, with town squares, blacksmiths and churches. Others re-create science-fiction and fairy-tale settings, like C.S. Lewis' Narnia, Frank Herbert's Dune, and the universe of Star Trek. Massachusetts Institute of Technology researchers have built a MUD model of their famous Media Lab, with offices and corridors corresponding to the real thing. One intrepid group of computer users constructed a section of the London Underground, complete with a virtual subway.[2]

Using MUD software commands, players are able to speak, move, and generally interact with others who have logged on to the site. Many find the experience highly addictive, and there are cases where students have logged on to a MUD for periods of up to eight hours in a single session.

This fact has not been lost on some educators, who have started to use these virtual environments to take advantage of the energy and interest shown by kids of all ages. In Cambridge, Massachusetts, for example, an educational MUD has been set up for elementary students. Using the MUD, a nine-year-old boy who had been to Yellowstone Park for a summer vacation built a working model of his trip instead of writing an essay about it.

Keep in mind this was all done with "words" only, but MUDs are being created with visual elements also. One virtual reality game known as Doom incorporates not only graphics but also sound, and multiple users on a network can play the game. It can also be played over the Internet. Flight simulators, such as Airwar, are other popular multiple-user games that contain high-resolution graphics and sound.

In the near future, when scarce bandwidth is not such a problem, it will probably be a common experience to enter numerous types of virtual realities that are multidimensional. Meantime, though, we can practice our literary skills and interact with others around the globe in real time on the traditional MUDs, or we can hop around in the digital "reality" of the World Wide Web.

Just-for-Fun Sites

Because Web is the most advanced protocol running on the Internet, text, sound, graphics, and video can be combined (though somewhat clumsily) to give us a taste of the Information Superhighway of the future. In addition, as people experiment with the possibilities for making money, teaching others, lobbying for causes, publishing their views, or supporting world democracy on the Web, some imaginative and entertaining resources have been made available to the intrepid Internet surfer.

With a Web browser loaded in the computer and a list of URLs in hand, you can take a quick tour of some of the I-Way's more playful stops. First destination: the Yahoo list at

    http://www.yahoo.com

Yahoo stands for "Yet Another Hierarchical Officious Oracle," which in itself is more whimsical than meaningful. But the Yahoo list is a truly helpful catalog of WWW sites, one of many organized listings of places to go on the Internet. The Yahoo list is maintained by David Filo and Jerry Yang, who began it as their personal list of favorite destinations while they were students at Stanford University.

When you access Yahoo, whose Home Page is shown on page 82, use your pointer to click on **Entertainment**, which activates a command to display another page of hyperlinked text of entertainment categories, ranging from Advice Columns and Amusement Parks to Travel and Virtual Reality. The number of resources are noted in parentheses beside each category.

Perhaps you'd like to know something about movies and films. If you click on that category, you'd find numerous options that will link you to other sites, or you can access the sites independently. Suppose you want to get clips of *Batman*. Go to:

`http://batmanforever.com`

Or you might go to a Casper-the-Friendly-Ghost site at

`http://www.mca.com`

Disney has a well-developed site with plenty of still pictures and video clips of movies such as the widely popular *Pocahontas* and *Lion King* that can be downloaded to your computer. For the *Lion King* there is also a section called "The Production Story," which tells how the movie was created.

Perhaps you are planning a trip to the famous Disneyland theme park in California or to its sister park in Florida? You can type in the URL

`http://www.best.com/~dijon/disney/parks/disneyland`

If all systems are go on the Internet, you should be presented with the Home Page of Disneyland , as it appears on page 83.

You might decide not to visit the Magic Kingdom after all. A little too tame, you say? Then go to the Big Apple for some real adventure. Enter:

`http://www.mediabridge.com/nyc/`

and select **Paperless Guide to NYC**. You'll see the Home Page as shown on page 84.

This commercial page has links to hundreds of resource files about the city. You might want to know about the admission fee for the Guggenheim Museum or its hours of operation. If you click on that text pointer, your screen will appear as it does on page 85.

As long as you're in the Big Apple, use your Web vehicle to cruise to upstate New York and travel back to 1994 and the festival that was held in Woodstock. The Internet address:

`http://www.well.com/woodstock/`

This interactive I-Way on-ramp, as shown on page 86, was created during the Woodstock '94 event using the resources of the WELL, the Whole Earth 'Lectronic Link, which runs a very active on-line service out of the San Francisco Bay Area with gateways to the Information Superhighway. As the text indicates, many people participated in the project, which was accessible throughout the world while it was happening in August 1994. Today you can go back to those days and try to relive the experience through the words and pictures of some of the people on the scene.

One popular band that was missing at Woodstock '94 was the Rolling Stones. But as long as you have access to the Web, you have access to information about rock and roll's traditional bad boys. In conjunction with their 1994 North American tour you can find out all about the band at

`http://www.stones.com`

The Rolling Stones Web Site Home Page appears on page 87. The reason for this page is obvious: promoters want to sell you the Stones. However, like many other commercial Internet experiments that offer some free services such as surveys and databases, this one offers a free resource, the MBONE software. With the software you can download a concert (audio) of the Stones' live performance at the Dallas Cotton Bowl. Unfortunately, this entails a huge amount of digital data, and very few personal computers have that much storage space, but the service is one more indicator of what we all can expect once the Information Superhighway is paved and ready for heavy traffic.

There are also some "time-waster" Home Pages that use the audio capabilities available in most of today's PCs. One is "Blue Dog Can Count" at

```
http://hp8.ini.cmu.edu:5550/bdf.html
```

If you type in two numbers and choose either to add or multiply, Blue Dog will actually send down an audio file of the correct number in dog language. He barks.

A Sign of Things to Come

Entertainment sites are still in the earliest stages of development, but they show what kind of impact the Net and the I-Way will have as the world begins to access an incredible array of information sources. Even now, for every silly Home Page available on the Web, there are at least a hundred well-planned and useful ones. Of the thousands of pages available today we can choose addresses like

```
http://www.cyberstore.ca/greenpeace/index.html
```

and access Greenpeace International and articles, graphics, and notices about this global environmental organization. Try

```
http://www.tollfree.att.net./dir800
```

which is the directory for AT&T 800 numbers.

An AIDS patent database that contains full text and illustrations of more than 1,500 patents related to AIDS diagnostics and drugs can be found at

`http://patents.cnidr.org`

Or you can always go for another pizza—but this time not from Pizza Hut. Try the following address instead, and you will see the Home Page shown below:

`http://www2.ecst.csuchico.edu/~pizza`

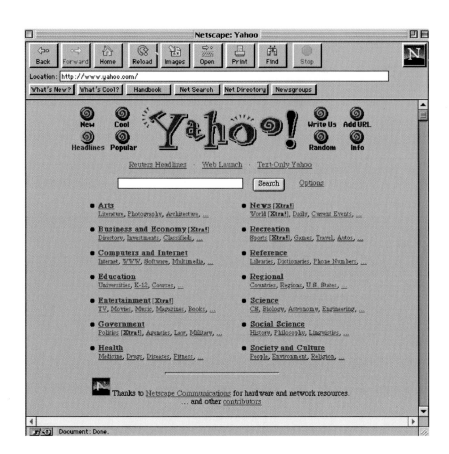

Disneyland Park

Planning Your Trip

- General Information
- Park Operating Schedule
- Directions to the Park
- Passport Prices
- Annual Passport Blackout Dates
- Disneyland FAQ

Within the Park

- Disneyland Park Map *(133, 759 bytes)*
- Disneyland Attractions
- Disneyland Shops
- Disneyland Restaurants and Refreshments
- *NEW!* Disneyland Entertainment Schedule *NEW!*

Miscellaneous

- The Marabic Page
- Souvenir Smashed Pennies
- Disneyland Skyway's Final Night
- Disneyland 40th Anniversary Collectors' Cards
- Disneyland Restroom Locations
- Disneyland Recipes

dijon@info.com

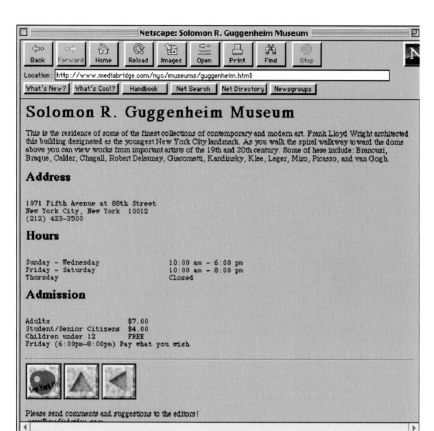

Solomon R. Guggenheim Museum

This is the residence of some of the finest collections of contemporary and modern art. Frank Lloyd Wright architected this building designated as the youngest New York City landmark. As you walk the spiral walkway toward the dome above you can view works from important artists of the 19th and 20th century. Some of hese include: Brancusi, Braque, Calder, Chagall, Robert Delaunay, Giacometti, Kandinsky, Klee, Leger, Miro, Picasso, and van Gogh.

Address

```
1071 Fifth Avenue at 88th Street
New York City, New York 10012
(212) 423-3500
```

Hours

```
Sunday - Wednesday          10:00 am - 6:00 pm
Friday - Saturday           10:00 am - 8:00 pm
Thursday                    Closed
```

Admission

```
Adults                  $7.00
Student/Senior Citizens $4.00
Children under 12       FREE
Friday (6:00pm-8:00pm) Pay what you wish
```

Please send comments and suggestions to the editors!

Back | Forward | Home | Reload | Images | Open | Print | Find | Stop

Netsite: http://www.well.com/woodstock/

What's New? | What's Cool? | Handbook | Net Search | Net Directory | Newsgroups

The Woodstock '94 Internet Multimedia Center

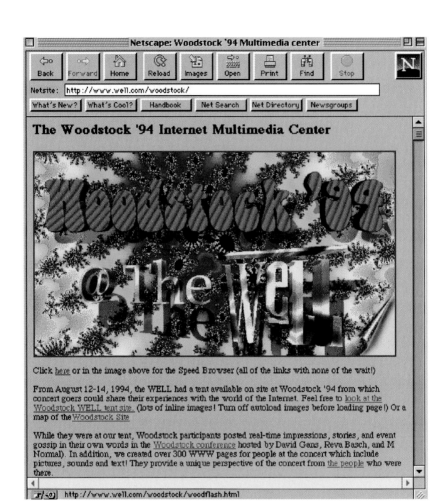

Click here or in the image above for the Speed Browser (all of the links with none of the wait!)

From August 12-14, 1994, the WELL had a tent available on site at Woodstock '94 from which concert goers could share their experiences with the world of the Internet. Feel free to look at the Woodstock WELL tent site. (lots of inline images! Turn off autoload images before loading page!) Or a map of the Woodstock Site

While they were at our tent, Woodstock participants posted real-time impressions, stories, and event gossip in their own words in the Woodstock conference hosted by David Gans, Reva Basch, and M Normal). In addition, we created over 300 WWW pages for people at the concert which include pictures, sounds and text! They provide a unique perspective of the concert from the people who were there.

http://www.well.com/woodstock/woodflash.html

The Official Rolling Stones Web Site

Check the new additions page. You are caller number **0876664**.
The Rolling Stones are on tour! Check the dates for your town!

If privacy is outlawed, only outlaws will have privacy.

—Phil Zimmerman, cryptography consultant

*P*roblems on the I-Way

Whether I-Way travelers are enjoying entertainment, learning new skills, searching for information, or uploading data, it is clear that more and more interaction is taking place digitally. This heavy traffic is creating some problems. One such problem is the ease with which con artists, thieves, perverts, and other crooks can prey on unsuspecting computer users. Another concern, which has been widely publicized, is the content of various messages and images transmitted on the Internet that some users and government regulators believe are pornographic, violent, or dangerous to public safety. One more worry is the encroachment on personal privacy by advertisers, government agencies, and political groups that collect data on people's lifestyles and habits.

Quite a different concern centers on the millions of people in the United States—and around the globe for that matter—who are *not* wired. Lack of access to cyberspace could result in a huge gap between those who can obtain data beneficial to their well-being and those who are left out of that loop. Such a gap could have adverse economic and social ramifications.

Piracy on the Internet

As it stands now, any digital information that travels along the network can be captured by avid computer users, generally referred to as "hackers," who have the right hardware and appropriately configured software. A few hackers (although certainly not the majority) have been involved in theft, fraud, and piracy on the Internet.

It is an easy task for hackers to "capture" a credit card number, name, and expiration date if that information is sent over the Internet to purchase compact discs, books, flowers, or other products. Then hackers use the stolen number to order merchandise and have it sent to their post office boxes. To avoid detection, the thieves use the box for several days and then move on to another address.

Telephone credit card numbers and computer programs are also targets of thieves. Phone numbers and programs are sold via the Internet and computer bulletin boards. In 1994, for example, twenty-two-year-old Max Louran was arrested for and later pleaded guilty to charges of "masterminding a plot to sell 140,000 pilfered phone-card numbers in the United States and abroad," according to a report in *Newsweek*.[1]

A November 1994 news feature in the *San Jose Mercury News* described how pirates operate. In one instance, an employee of a San Rafael, California, computer-game company helped a software piracy group in the Pacific Northwest filch one of the latest computer games, TIE Fighter. The employee sent the program via modem and computer to the head of the ring, a woman named Jenny. When Jenny received the program, it lacked the code keys needed to play the game without an owner's manual. That was hardly a problem, however. According to the news report:

> Jenny then dialed into the Internet, the global computer network, and after taking several deliberate electronic detours, she connected with a small computer in Moscow. There, a programming whiz who goes by the name "Skipjack" quickly cracked the codes and sent the program back across the Internet to "Waves of Warez," a Seattle bulletin board popular with software pirates. Within 24 hours, "TIE Fighter" would be

available to thousands of software pirates in major cities worldwide—days before its official release date.[2]

Another computer hacker, Kevin Mitnick, was arrested in 1995 in Raleigh, North Carolina, after being on the run from the law since 1992. Mitnick had been arrested in 1988 for pilfering thousands of credit card numbers, none of which he ever used. A longtime hacker, he apparently has been obsessed with proving his technical abilities.

Mitnick was sentenced to federal prison in 1988 but was placed on probation with the stipulation that he not use a computer or modem. He continued his activities, however, and managed to work past security codes to break into the computer files of Tsutomu Shimomura, a highly respected computer security expert in Del Mar, California. Mitnick stole databases, documents, and software programs from Shimomura, but his theft was soon discovered. Shimomura traced Mitnick's activities via computer, the Net, and cellular modem, which eventually led to Mitnick's arrest by the FBI.[3]

Copyright Controversies

In the future, piracy probably won't be limited to software and phone-card numbers; numerous products and services will be offered on the Internet and could be subject to theft. Government efforts are underway to protect some electronic property rights by amending the Copyright Act, but this has led to great controversy. Users who regularly communicate over the Internet believe in sharing whatever materials they might find in cyberspace, although they certainly don't condone the sale of stolen software and credit card numbers.

During 1993, a Working Group on Intellectual Property Rights of the NII examined ways to revamp the copyright law and issued a preliminary report in 1994. This report has generated varied opinions from legal scholars and Internet users. Some insist that the Working Group's definitions of the law will make virtually all electronic activities violations of copyright law. Others believe that amendments to the copyright law are needed to provide more stringent protection and ensure that those who produce text materials, recordings, and images/graphics are able to maintain control of their works.

In a related lawsuit filed in February 1995, the Church of Scientology (COS) of California sued Dennis Erlich, a former member and now a critic of the church. COS claimed Erlich illegally published literary works that belonged to the COS by transmitting them over the Internet. Because Erlich posted portions of published and unpublished works of Scientology founder L. Ron Hubbard on a newsgroup, the church also sued the Internet provider and operator of the electronic bulletin board (**alt.religion.scientology**), claiming all had infringed the copyright law. The court at first issued a restraining order requiring the defendants to stop publication of the Hubbard documents. But Netcom, the Internet provider, argued that COS had demanded "an unprecedented extension of [copyright] infringement liability," and if the court recognized this, millions of Internet users would be affected.

In fact, Netcom does not maintain databases or other content but is simply a computer program that allows subscribers to issue commands to log on to the Internet. And the newsgroup is one of hundreds of bulletin boards, any one of which could distribute the Hubbard materials. Prohibiting Netcom and similar services from operating would "fundamentally alter the functioning of the world's largest electronic public library and potentially expose each of its millions of users to unlimited tort liability," Netcom lawyers argued.

Eventually the court dropped the order against the Internet provider and operator of the newsgroup and ruled that the restraining order against Erlich did *not* prohibit fair use of the works of L. Ron Hubbard. Fair use, the court said, "includes use of the copyrighted work for the purpose of criticism, news reporting, teaching, scholarship, and research."[4]

Privacy Concerns

Because so much information travels back and forth on the I-Way, the possibility of someone tracking this data or breaking into government networks or company databanks to obtain personal information becomes very real. Hackers, for example, have tampered with U.S. government computers.

One reason hackers invade government networks is to prove to themselves (as was the case with Mitnick) that they have mastered computer skills. Hackers also want to demonstrate that authorities are vulnerable. Their intent is not necessarily to steal secret information. Nevertheless, some hackers have created havoc, taking control of several U.S. military computer systems. They have altered or erased files or shut systems down, which has adversely affected military readiness.

Another problem that concerns privacy advocates is the potential for abuse in tracking consumers' online interests, purchases, and inquiries. The most-used online commercial service, America Online (AOL), which has more than 2.5 million subscribers with one million connections every day, was marketing its subscriber database to direct mail companies. AOL claimed it was only providing names and addresses, but the company has access to a great deal of information about its subscribers.

Some members of the U.S. Congress have been pressuring commercial online service providers to adopt standards for protecting subscribers' privacy. As a result, in October 1994, AOL agreed to stop releasing subscriber information and announced that the company is working with other groups "to establish an industrywide privacy and ethical practices code."[5]

The government's Office of Technology Assessment (OTA) has studied the privacy issue and released a report that is available on the Net at

`ftp://otabbs.ota.gov/pub/information.security`

Called "Information Security and Privacy in Network Environments," the report deals with the vulnerability of the Internet and other networks where people worldwide exchange messages. It also points out that "every day U.S. banks transfer about $1 trillion among themselves, and New York markets trade an average of $2 trillion in securities. Nearly all of these transactions pass over information networks."[6] The OTA focuses on safeguarding this information and supports encryption technology—a coding system.

The Clipper Chip

The U.S. government plan for a coding system is the Escrowed Encryption Standard (EES)—also known as the Clipper chip—which was announced in 1993 when lawmakers were attempting to rewrite the sixty-year-old telecommunications regulations. The Clipper chip generates special encryption software that turns data into unreadable secret code. This type of encryption would also provide law enforcement officials with computer software "keys" to decode messages—if they are authorized to use what would be the equivalent of a wiretap.

Already AT&T is manufacturing phones that incorporate the Clipper chip—it applies an encryption to outgoing calls and decodes on the other end with the same chip installed in the callee's phone. The federal government wants all data transmitted on the Internet to be so encoded. However, the National Security Council, the Federal Bureau of Investigation, and other government agencies would be able to request the "key" to unlock the code for the encryption should they feel that an individual might be dealing in illegal data transmission, such as sending bomb instructions or child pornography over the networks.

Although avid I-Way users do not support illegal activities on the Internet, they were outraged when the Clipper chip was proposed. The core group that helped develop the protocols and the many uses for digital communication asked what kind of privacy protection citizens could expect if the government had the means to track their communications and transactions. In their view, the U.S. Internal Revenue Service would use this "Big Brother" tool to track the increasing number of currency transactions moving along the networks. In short, longtime users of the Net believe that all communication should be private, and that users must be free to establish their own encryption, such as the freely available PGP, or Pretty Good Privacy.

After the government announcement about the Clipper chip,

arguments and discussions raged for months on network Usenet news-groups, mail lists, forums, and thousands of local electronic bulletin board systems. At first, the Clinton administration seemed to back off, but legislation requiring some kind of encryption is still pending.

One thing is certain: Net users are not giving up this fight. Groups such as the Electronic Frontier Foundation (EFF) and Computer Professionals for Social Responsibility (CPSR) along with online journals like *Red Rock Eater* (RRE), *Computer underground Digest* (CuD), *Computer PRIVACY Digest* (CPD), *Computers and Academic Freedom* (CAF), *Cypherpunks*, and *CyberWire Dispatch* keep the issue on the front burner with organized e-mail write-in campaigns, press releases, opinion pieces, and informational workshops. As reported in *Time*,

> a large part of the problem is cultural. The rules that govern behavior on the Net were set by computer hackers who largely eschew formal rules. Instead, most computer wizards subscribe to a sort of anarchistic ethic, stated most succinctly in Steven Levy's *Hackers*. Among its tenets:
> - Access to computers should be unlimited and total.
> - All information should be free.
> - Mistrust authority and promote decentralization.[7]

Hate, Obscenity, and Pornography

Although the wealth of resources and information accessible on the Net can provide huge advantages and many educational opportunities, the virtual world is very much a reflection of the real one. Individuals and groups may use the Internet—as they have used more traditional means of communication—to spread hate messages, advocate violence, or distribute pornography. Some militia groups in the United States and Canada, for example, have used the Internet as a rapid means of distributing their messages advocating the extermination of Jews, blacks, and others whom they consider "unfit" for association with the dominant white society in North America.

Pornography is a definite concern, particularly as students begin to enter cyberspace. For example, a couple in Milpitas, California, distributed what was deemed "obscene" material over a bulletin board system. In 1994, a hacker in Memphis, Tennessee, broke into the couple's system and later complained to authorities. A federal court determined that the material was obscene according to standards of the locale—Memphis—where the images were received, and the couple faces a prison term and hefty fines for transmitting obscenity over interstate phone lines, although the case has been appealed.

Pornography is also accessible at some Usenet newsgroups. In a controversial move, in December 1995 CompuServe obeyed an order by the German government to block member access to 200 newsgroups the government deemed pornographic. This move affected CompuServe users in 140 countries and was the first time any government had taken drastic action to limit public access to the Internet. But it caused such an uproar that CompuServe quickly restored access and decided to work on a way to limit it only in Germany.

However, "finding smut on the Net is nothing like flicking a remote control at a cable box—you have to know where to look," wrote Steven Levy in a column for *Newsweek*. Levy is adamantly opposed to censorship of the Net.

Yet Levy and many other Internet users agree that schools and parents should be able to protect children from the portrayal of violence and sexually explicit content in the general media. Many school districts have policies and procedures in place regarding possession of offending material in *any* medium. If a copy of a hard-core sex magazine is being passed around the school, the principal has a set of well-established guidelines to deal with the problem. Students may face a variety of penalties ranging from detention to suspension from school. If there is a transgression involving the Internet, one disciplinary action may be to revoke the student's computer account.

Some schools (and parents at home) may opt for a product called SurfWatch or similar software. Introduced in 1995 by Surf-Watch Software, the company describes its product as a "breakthrough . . . that helps you deal with the flood of sexually explicit material on the Internet . . . blocking what is being received at any individual computer." Similar to the parental controls available on television subscription services, the software was designed to block material from newsgroups, FTP and gopher sites, and WWW pages that educators and parents consider objectionable.

Critics of the software charged, however, that the SurfWatch filter blocked any material that related to homosexuality or bisexuality, which included information and education about these lifestyles, even though there was and is no explicit sexual material involved. Some Internet users argued that SurfWatch would be just one of a number of self-proclaimed guardians of the Internet, imposing the company's values on the worldwide community. But as the company heard from critics it adopted a policy to set up formal relationships with advisers who can help them distinguish between sexually explicit materials and those that simply pertain to sexual minority communities.

Out of the Loop

Whatever the problems on the Net, they mean little to those who have no access to it. The national information infrastructure vision, as delineated by Vice President Gore, addresses the very important issue of the "haves" and "have nots" of information technology. Like telephone service, the vice president and community activists are insisting that the principle of "universal access" be applied to the Information Superhighway. After all, how can the initiatives for online democracy evolve if the only people with a vote or the ones with the ability to express an opinion are those with enough money and/or technical ability to have and use the equipment of connectivity? Obviously, people can be left out of the loop.

A report on the United States' Latino population released in September 1994 and forwarded to the Internet population points out the problems of gaining access for one particular subgroup in the United States. Written by Anne Larson and Anthony Wilhelm, the report "Latinos and the Information Superhighway" notes that

By the year 2050, Latinos will constitute over 20 percent of the nation's population. Currently, 29.3 percent of Latinos live under the poverty level, while the percentage of low-income Latino households with telephones is well below the national average of 94.2 percent. These statistics suggest that the development and education of low-income persons is crucial for America's future. . . . Unless Latinos have access to information technology, many will be barred from the information highway—as consumers, as producers of information, and as political participants. In a market-driven highway, the balance between treatment of information as a commodity, and treatment of information as a resource of political and social value, is much harder to maintain.[8]

Latino families living below the poverty line obviously have a problem purchasing computers, modems, software, and connections to the information services. Accordingly, "only about 9.6 percent of Hispanic households own a personal computer (February 15, 1993) while the figure for all homes and small businesses is over 30."[9]

For many "have nots" (such as the homeless in the United States), owning the equipment and receiving the training are very real problems. About the only place many people actually get their hands on the technology is in schools or at the library. Seattle Public Library was one of the first to provide free hookups to the Internet, and many homeless people have taken advantage of this opportunity to discover and use resources ranging from bulletin boards and games to data banks listing job openings. A few homeless shelters in major cities also offer this type of service.

Will that be sufficient for "universal access" of the data and the power? That is one of the issues, among many, being debated today. The potential for everyone to get on the Information Superhighway exists: engineers are continually making computers easier to use, and costs are dropping by half every eighteen months. But the I-Way will only function for all if the majority of the people stay actively engaged in monitoring its development.

The civic life of the citizens of cyberspace may consist of purer, less bigoted interactions than those that . . . take place among citizens interacting face to face. . . . The civic life of cyberspace may represent a higher order of democracy.

—report presented at the Annual Meeting of the American Political Science Association

Virtual Community

The I-Way must always be considered in the context of real, life-altering change that is affecting the entire planet. The technological advances that have accelerated those changes must be understood by the individual if he or she is to achieve some sort of equilibrium with the spinning events, the overpowering information, and loss of "the old ways." Peter von Stackelberg describes the situation this way:

> The digital revolution will fundamentally reshape the world. It will be a much faster, more rapidly changing world. It will be a world in which much of what we hear, see and feel (perhaps even smell and taste) will be subjected to digital manipulation. We will experience a world in which it will become increasingly difficult to identify the difference between reality and virtual reality. Sensory . . . boundaries that have been in place for the entire existence of the human species will become more and more blurred over the next 20 to 40 years. The students of today and tomorrow will have to become increasingly adept at deciphering what they see, hear and feel in order to determine what is reality and what is not.

Often, they will need to decide what they want their reality to be from amongst a variety of choices.

The soft skills (communication, team work, personal leadership, and so on) will be increasingly important as they will serve as the components of the moral, emotional, spiritual and psychological gyroscope that we will all need in order to navigate through changing, turbulent and conflicting realities.[1]

Meet the Future

What is the reality of the future? How will concepts like democracy and community evolve when the manner in which we relate to one another changes so dramatically? Is your neighborhood the street where you live, or does it become the online members of the listserv from which you receive and send e-mail five times a day? Or will it be defined as your favorite interactive TV show that you become addicted to in the year 2001? These may seem like silly questions to some, but they are important considerations when we observe the way institutions and "life as usual" are currently shifting.

Not long ago our interaction was mostly local; issues were discussed with the people down the street. Then telephones greatly enhanced our ability to touch base with others in various locales who also had an instrument connected to the line. Eventually, television and radio gave us common access to information from around the world. Now, the Information Superhighway and its precursor, the Internet, have the potential to empower all who can get on board.

Many of these changes are a direct result of the expanding ability of individuals to access information and then to communicate their feelings about that information to a wider audience. A report from the University of Missouri puts these developments into an interesting perspective:

Tens of thousands of years ago, humans stumbled upon the gift of language. For most of the generations that followed, change crept at a glacial pace; so slowly that an individual could hardly notice it inching along. For a peasant in China, say, or in the Balkans, life in the 16th century passed a lot like life in the 6th century. But in the last half-century, we've lived through more change than all the humans in all the 100,000 years before us.

To put it another way: If the time span of language could be crammed into a 24-hour day, most of the change would have happened in the day's final minute. Before then, people depended on the spoken word for information: spoken words laboriously handed down the chain of generations, link by link. Gradually, clusters of educated people froze the spoken word into symbols and handed them down on durable things; clay tablets, for example. The symbols slowly evolved into letters and the things into paper. Suddenly, the printing press began spewing out words with a speed and reach that unsettled the world. But the real revolution rolled in with our own century, when:

- Radio let millions hear new information.
- Television let millions see new information.
- The personal computer let millions control new information.[2]

Manifestations of the Change

Politics is a key indicator of the way life is changing in the United States. Most politicians try to build a consensus within their constituencies in order to wield power. Power, for good or evil, is the goal of the political life. Despots do this with brute force and intimidation and by controlling the information to which their subjects are exposed, frightening the masses into giving up their power. Modern high-tech campaigns, designed to elect nominees to important offices in America, spend as much as a million dollars a week on the broadcast media to sway public opinion toward their causes. The tone of some of the negative personal attacks might even lead one to believe that the idea is to "scare" citizens into voting against one party, thereby ensuring that the other will receive the power.

The dictator and the democrat both know that the surest way to stay on top in the political game is to control information. Sometimes that means keeping the facts hidden; sometimes it means perpetuating the plausible lie. Unfortunately, most governments occasionally resort to keeping their citizens in the dark, for "their own good." Translated, that means they maintain control.

Thomas Jefferson pointed out long ago that a nation must guard against ignorance if it expects to be free, and that every American has the responsibility to be informed. In President Jefferson's time, knowledge was spread by word of mouth and the earliest newspapers. Today, digital communications tools spread the latest information across the globe faster than it took you to read this paragraph, and with the advent of the I-Way, government shortcomings are a lot easier to find. How does that relate to power and control?

Peter von Stackelberg of Applied Futures explains it this way:

> Information is moving control within organizations from a centralized to a decentralized paradigm. Because of the complexity and rapid rate of change both within and outside of our business and governmental organizations, centralized control is becoming less and less effective. For these organizations to survive, they must be able to move control/decision making to the "front lines."[3]

To their credit, many leaders in the U.S. government have seen the importance of developing the communication tools that will give ordinary citizens the power to access information and make informed choices. They also have provided improved methods to get a message back to the people who are sitting in the positions of trust. The Clinton administration and members of Congress from both parties helped create the vision of the National Information Infrastructure. Within that concept are initiatives to create standards for making data available, providing universal access to the Information Superhighway, making certain that private information remains private, and so on.

The most visible leadership has come from the technological team within the White House, which has experimented with all the new protocols since the beginning of the Clinton presidency. Clinton is the first sitting president to send e-mail to citizens—a group of fifth graders—and Vice President Gore was the first vice president in office to conduct an online computer conference. The administration's efforts also include establishment of an electronic self-service public document library that can be reached by e-mail at

`publications@whitehouse.gov`

California may be the most ambitious state government in its efforts to allow citizens to access much of the information it controls. After a great deal of online electronic lobbying by citizens' groups, the state legislature in 1994 passed the first bill in the nation requiring state offices to provide for electronic access to a broad cross section of the data they collect. By the end of the year, the state provided live, online election results and pre- and postelection results. Anyone with Internet access could address

`http://www.election.ca.gov/`

or

`gopher.elections.ca.gov`

California's general election returns in November 1994 were presented in graphical, tabular formats, making this the largest live online Internet project undertaken. Following the election, people were able to obtain detailed summary data on the voting results.

Grassroots Developments

Ordinary citizens, though, are the ones who have been using the new medium to organize and educate their peers in some interesting and effective ways. Grassroots networks provide all types of traditional community services through the FreeNet concept developed by Tom Grunder and National Public Telecomputing Network. The Youngstown (Ohio) FreeNet, for example, provides information about city government, places of worship, hospitals, Youngstown State University, and other local institutions.

Volunteers have donated their time and resources to establish electronic databases designed to ensure that impartial information is available to voters about issues, events, and candidates seeking office. They use such electronic tools as the WWW and the other Internet protocols to "publish" and send out information. Unlike the past when the power of the press belonged to those who owned a press, today "On the Web, everyone with the necessary skills owns a press," as John December wrote in his book, *The World Wide Web Unleashed*. He emphasized that

> dissemination of ideas on a mass and medium scale is no longer filtered through organizations and institutions but can come directly from individuals. Net and Web-based magazines (zines) can flourish . . . this is a dramatic shift from institutions as holders of the publishing key.[4]

One grassroots publishing effort worth noting is Project Vote Smart, which is based in Corvallis, Oregon. This organization set up a WWW Home Page at

`http://www.oclc.org/VoteSmart/lwv/lwvhome.htm`

The general public can obtain data the group compiled on people running for elected office throughout the United States. Hundreds of volunteers have assembled factual information on more than two thousand candidates, including candidates for the 1996 presidential election. If you access the site, you can find information on who has paid for candidates' campaigns, the voting records of those in office, telephone numbers and mailing addresses of office seekers, and so forth.

Another citizen-activist effort of note, and another first, was achieved in the state of Minnesota when the Electronic Democracy Project staged the first two online debates between candidates for governor and those running for the senate. Through the use of mail list software, citizens could subscribe to an e-mail exchange between the participants, which lasted for several days in October and November of 1994. Even if a resident wasn't subscribed, an archive of the exchanges was available immediately after the events. Voters could then read the information at their convenience before voting. According to the organizers, the project "created a space on-line for the distribution of candidate position papers, and other information pertaining to the 1994 election season in Minnesota." [5]

Numerous electronic projects tackle "global village" concerns such as human rights abuses, threats to the environment, and news censorship. PeaceNet, a global network of activists working for peace around the world, began in 1984 in San Francisco, expanding rapidly to seven hundred subscribers within a year. Now dozens of organizations concerned about nuclear arms proliferation and human-rights abuses post messages and calls for action on PeaceNet.

PeaceNet spawned similar networks—EcoNet, ConflictNet, LaborNet, and WomensNet—which are now under one umbrella, the Institute for Global Communications (IGC), with membership totaling more than 10,000. IGC networks and others like them around the world are frequently able to call attention to problems and issues that might otherwise remain hidden, such as repressive legislation, imprisonment of political activists, and hazards to the environment. Activists are alerted to actions they can take—sending faxes, writing letters, calling reporters, joining protest marches—and their quick response can help change the course of events.

In the future, there will be many more imaginative uses of the I-Way to further the development of democracy, protect the global environment, and assure the health, safety, and civil rights of citizens throughout the connected world. But these lofty goals depend on the free flow of information, which U.S.-based groups such as the Electronic Freedom Foundation and the Computer Users for Social Responsibility well understand. These organizations and others work to safeguard open and equal access to the I-Way worldwide and to ensure that in the United States the NII "empowers citizens, protects individual rights, and strengthens the democratic institutions on which this country was founded."[6]

Source Notes

1

1. Stan Davis and Bill Davidson, *2020 Vision* (New York: Simon & Schuster), 1991, 16–17.
2. "Digital Technology," *The New Grolier Multimedia Encyclopedia*, Release 6 (Danbury, Conn.: Grolier), 1993.

2

1. Albert Gore Jr., "Information Superhighways: The Next Information Revolution," *Futurist*, Jan–Feb 1991, 21.
2. Vice President Al Gore, National Press Club, December 21, 1993, The White House **75300.3115@compuserve.com**
3. "Info Chips," *Seattle Times*, April 17, 1994, D6.
4. FAQ on the NII, **gopher@ntiaunix1.ntia.doc.gov**
5. Michael Antonoff et al., "The Complete Survival Guide to the Information Superhighway," *Popular Science*, May 1994, 105.
6. Michael Burgi, "No U Turn," *Mediaweek*, April 19, 1993, 26–30.
7. Andy Reinhardt, "Building the Data Highway," *Byte*, March 1994, 48–49.
8. Quoted in "Tech News," *Seattle Times*, May 1, 1994, D2.
9. Charles Piller, "Dreamnet," *Macworld*, October 1994, 102.
10. "U S West Marketing," *Business Wire* electronic press release, September 26, 1994.
11. Paul Andrews, "Multimedia Wizard," *Seattle Times*. October 24, 1994, D2.
12. Robert W. Lucky, "Keeping the Faith in Technology," *Chicago Tribune*, Perspective Section, 23.

3

1. Vice President Al Gore, National Press Club, December 21, 1993, The White House **75300.3115@compuserve.com**
2. "The National Information Infrastructure: Agenda for Action," September 1993, 2; electronic version at gopher server: **ace.esusda.gov**
3. Ibid.
4. From First Virtual Home Page at **http://www.fv.com/**
5. From a DigiCash Home Page at **http://www.digicash.com**

4

1. Quoted in Bernard Aboba, "The Birth of the ARPANET," *The Online User's Encyclopedia*, Addison-Wesley, November 1993. Available from **gopher://is.internic.net/00/infoguide/about-internet /history/aboba-cerf**
2. Quoted in Michael Hauben, "Behind the Net: The Untold History of the ARPANET," **gopher://gopher.cic.net/00/e-serials/alphabetic/a/amateur computerist/netboo k/ch.6_untold_ARPA.gz**
3. Networld+Interop 94 Tokyo 27–29 July 1994 Keynote Address, "The Present and the Future of the Internet: Five Faces," by Anthony-Michael Rutkowski, executive director, Internet Society, **http://info.isoc.org/interop-tokyo.html**

5

1. Internet Info, Falls Church, Va. Note: For more information e-mail to **info@internetinfo.com**
2. Rick Tetzeli, "The Internet and Your Business," *Fortune*, March 7, 1994, 86.
3. Adam Engst, *Internet Starter Kit for the Mac* (Indianapolis, Ind.: Hayden Books, 1993), 18.
4. Cathy Reiner, "Your Dream Home, On-Line," *Seattle Times*, May 29, 1994, G1.

6

1. Brenda C. Coleman, "Three-D Cadaver Seen on Internet," Associated Press, November 28, 1994.
2. Quoted in Howard Dukes, "Riley High Adds to Superhighway," *South Bend Tribune*, June 11, 1995, C6.
3. Quoted in "Follow that Butterfly," *NEA Today*, May 1995, 17.

7

1. Quoted in James Sinks, "Teachers Want High-Tech Help," *Register-Guard*, July 29, 1994, reprinted electronic mail list SUPERK12, October 16, 1994.
2. Adam Engst, *Internet Starter Kit for the Mac* (Indianapolis, Ind.: Hayden Books, 1993), 374–421.
3. Rick Tetzeli, "The Internet and Your Business," *Fortune*, March 7, 1994, 88.

8

1. Edupage quoting *Investor's Business Daily*, September 9, 1994, A4.
2. Edupage quoting *NBC Nightly News*, March 22, 1994.
3. Edupage quoting *Miami Herald*, April 15, 1994, C1.
4. Peter von Stackelberg, e-mail correspondence with Martin Gay, October 25, 1994.
5. Ibid.
6. Ibid.

7. Daniel Marcus e-mail correspondence with Martin Gay, October 26, 1994.

8. Quoted in Steven Spenser, "Opportunities Abound in Multimedia," *Seattle Times*, October 16, 1994, Section J, 1–2.

9

1. Ellen Germain, "In the Jungle of MUD," *Time*, September 13, 1993, 61.

2. Ibid.

10

1. Michael Meyer with Anne Underwood, "Crimes on the 'Net,' " *Newsweek*, November 14, 1994, 47.

2. Adam S. Bauman, "How Pirates Use Internet to Steal, Spread Software," *San Jose Mercury News*, November 4, 1994, 1D.

3. Katie Hafner, "A Superhacker Meets His Match," *Newsweek*, February 27, 1995, 61–62.

4. Quoted in Jonathan Rosenoer, "To Silence a Critic," *CyberLaw*, April 1995, **http://www.portal.com/;~cyberlaw/cylw_home.html**

5. Edupage quoting *The Wall Street Journal*, October 26, 1994, B10.

6. "OTA Report on Information Security and Privacy," September 27, 1994.

7. David S. Jackson and Suneel Ratan, "Battle for the Soul of the Internet," *Time*, July 25, 1994, 50–56.

8. Anne Larson and Anthony Wilhelm, "Latinos and the Information Superhighway," the Tomas Rivera Center policy brief, September 1994, Scripps College, Claremont, Cal. Accessed on the internet via *Red Rock Eater* mail list, Phil Agre, October 27, 1994.

9. Ibid.

11

1. Peter von Stackelberg, e-mail correspondence with Martin Gay, October 25, 1994.

2. University of Missouri, *2020: A Vision for the Future*, January 5, 1994.

3. Peter von Stackelberg, e-mail correspondence with Martin Gay, October 25, 1994.

4. John December, "Challenges for a Webbed Society," *Computer-Mediated Communication Magazine*, November 1, 1994, 7.

5. G. Scott Aikens, **aikens@Free-Net.Mpls-StPaul.MN.US**, October 20, 1994, posted to Net-Happenings.

6. Executive Summary, "The NII: Serving the Community," Computer Professionals for Social Responsibility.

Further Reading

Badgett, Tom, and Corey Sandler. *Welcome to...Internet: From Mystery to Mastery.* New York: MIS: Press, 1993. 2d. ed., 1995.

Braun, Eric. *The Internet Directory.* New York: Fawcett Columbine, 1994.

Butler, Mark. *How to Use the Internet.* Emeryville, Calif.: Ziff-Davis Press, 1994.

Cogswell, Jeffrey M. *Simple Internet.* Corte Madera, Calif.: Waite Group Press, 1994.

Comer, Douglas E. *The Internet Book: Everything You Need to Know About Computer Networking and How the Internet Works.* Englewood Cliffs, N.J.: Prentice Hall, 1994.

Crumlish, Christian. *The Internet Dictionary: The Essential Guide to Netspeak.* Alameda, Calif.: SYBEX, Inc., 1995.

Engst, Adam C. *The Internet Starter Kit.* Indianapolis: Hayden Books, 1995.

Etings, Joshua. *How the Internet Works.* Emeryville, Calif.: Ziff-Davis Press, 1994.

Gookin, Dan, and Andy Rathbone. *PCs for Dummies.* 2d ed. San Mateo, Calif.: IDG Books, 1994.

Kane, Pamela. *Hitchhiker's Guide to the Electronic Highway.* New York: MIS: Press, 1994.

Kaynak, Joe, et al. *The First Book of Personal Computing.* 3d. ed. Carmel, Ind.: Alpha Books, 1992.

Kehoe, Brendan. *Zen and the Art of the Internet: A Beginner's Guide.* 3d. ed. Englewood Cliffs, N.J.: Prentice Hall, 1994.

LaQuey, Tracy, and J. C. Ryer. *The Internet Companion: A Beginner's Guide to Global Networking.* 2d. ed. Reading, Mass.: Addison-Wesley, 1994.

Lemay, Laura. *Teach Yourself Web Publishing with HTML in 14 Days.* Indianapolis: Sams Publishing, 1995.

Pedersen, Ted, and Francis Moss. *Internet for Kids! A Beginner's Guide to Surfing the Net.* Los Angeles: Price Stern Sloan, 1995.

Rose, Donald. *Minding Your Cybermanners on the Internet: An Entertaining Guide to the Do's and Don'ts of Life Online!* Indianapolis: Alpha Books, 1994.

Stoll, Clifford. *Silicon Snake Oil: Second Thoughts on the Information Highway.* New York: Doubleday, 1995.

Index